THE VOYAGE OF *SABRA*

The Voyage of
SABRA

✝✝✝✝✝✝

An Ecological Cruise through the Caribbean, with Extras

✝✝✝✝✝✝

MICHAEL L. FRANKEL

W.W. NORTON & COMPANY
New York   London

The text of this book is composed in Bembo. Composition by ComCom. Manufacturing by Haddon Craftsmen. Book design by Jacques Chazaud.

Library of Congress Cataloging-in-Publication Data
Frankel, Michael L.
    The voyage of SABRA : an ecological cruise through the Caribbean, with extras / Michael L. Frankel.
        p.   cm.
    ISBN 0-393-02852-6
    1. SABRA (Ship)   2. Scientific expeditions—Caribbean Area.   3. Natural history—Caribbean Area.   4.Man—Influence on nature—Caribbean Area.   5. Ecology—Caribbean Area.   6. Human ecology—Caribbean Area.   7. Marine biology—Caribbean Area.   I. Title.
QH11.F73   1990   90-37358
508.729—dc20   CIP
ISBN 0-393-02852-6

W.W. Norton & Company, Inc., 500 Fifth Avenue, New York, N.Y. 10110
W.W. Norton & Company, Ltd., 37 Great Russell Street, London WC1B 3NU

1 2 3 4 5 6 7 8 9 0

For

The many supporters of the work of the
Center for Marine Conservation and the
friends who encouraged me to go by
reminding me that between the dream and
the deed lie the doldrums.

PASSAGE

The waves murmur faint protest
as they part before the bow.

Foam hissing softly, they glide alongside,
disappearing astern into the night.

Gentle swings of the rudder
wash it in a softly-glowing phosphorescence.

An island of light
in the dark that surrounds,
the compass is steady, reassuring.

The sails curve taut and full.

The groan of mast, sigh of rigging, tremor of hull
articulate the embrace of boat, wind and water
that compels us forward.

We pass the hours over mugs of tea,
talking quietly—
of the day just passed,
of the lights of a far off ship,
of adventures known and longed-for,
of our fears and dreams.

Or we sleep, alternating,
curled in the cockpit,
lulled by the gentle rhythm of the boat
and our comfortable companionship.

The Southern Cross hangs suspended
off the starboard bow,
gradually slipping toward the horizon.

Stars beyond counting, dazzling in their multitudes,
arc their courses across the sky,
easing our way toward dawn.

We are friends,
sharing a night passage.

KIT ARMSTRONG

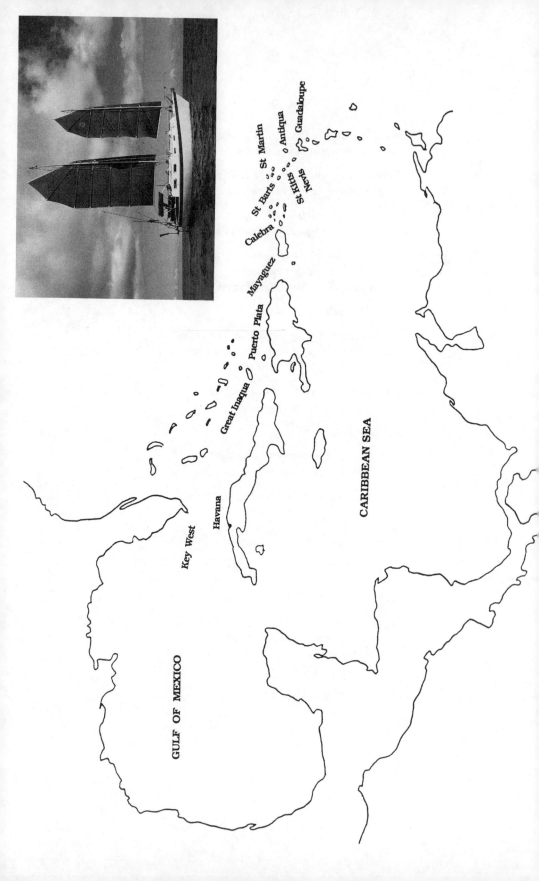

GULF OF MEXICO

Key West

Havana

CARIBBEAN SEA

Great Inagua

Puerto Plata

Mayaguez

Culebra

St Barts

St Martin

St Kitts

Nevis

Antigua

Guadaloupe

Contents

✝✝✝✝✝

Preface

✝✝✝✝✝

In the winter of 1987 *Sabra,* a 32-foot Chinese junk-rigged schooner, slipped her icebound mooring lines in Washington, D.C. and headed for the sunny Caribbean. The ensuing six-month voyage, sponsored by the Center for Marine Conservation, covered more than 5,000 miles and 22 islands. The voyage was a personal adventure capping my two-year tenure as the Chairman of the Center. It was also an opportunity to explore marine conservation issues firsthand, and through contact with local officials, regarding further research needs, public policy concerns, and the need for public education on the marine environment. My specific environmental areas of interest were: plastic debris in the ocean, marine sanctuaries and parks, threatened sea turtles, critical mangrove habitats, international trade in endangered species and species products, and boat anchor damage to sensitive coral and sea grass beds. The growth of tourism and tourist related development investments have made the Caribbean's sensitive marine environment an important focus for the Center's conservation goals.

I am indebted to many supporters and the Center's staff for the success of the voyage. Mary Adele Donnelly, Burr Heneman, and Michael Weber provided considerable research support on the many environmental issues I encountered in the Caribbean. Kathleen Armstrong provided an environmental law perspective and acted as the expedition poet. Merna Hurd, Raf Frankel, Scott Frankel, Ellison Burton, and Robert Burton joined me on various segments of the trip and were invaluable mates in helping sail *Sabra* from place to place so that we could explore as much of the environment as possible. I want to acknowledge the special support and guidance given by Roger McManus, the president of the Center.

Documenting the voyage was made all the more enjoyable by being able to share my logs with the many friends that I had badgered into supporting marine conservation and this project. Special thanks to Rebecca Hanmer, Mary Fowler, Adam and Ann Poe, Ann Randolph, Abe and Dorothy Shapiro, Regina and Nat Greenspan, Jerome and Marilyn Bracken, Howard and Kathleen Grossman, Paul and Betty Cinquegrana, Richard and Florence Bank, Sarah Kirchen, Yvonne and Donald Lewis, Freda Alpert, Scott Carlin, Dick and Germaine Swanson, Kathleen Calvert, Fred and Alice White, Francine Sanders, Chuck McLean and Amy Margerum, Bruce and Virginia Douglas, Gerald and Joan Doren, Bill Brown, Larry and Eve Barrett and Rick Kuder.

Sabra's log is interspersed with several environmental sidebar notes and illustrations taken from the Center's numerous educational publications. Hopefully, these notes, together with the photographs and the wildlife illustrations by Mary Beath and Jill Perry Townsend, will help to explain the complex environmental issues surrounding marine conservation.

Michael L. Frankel
Washington, D.C.

Breaking the Ice

✝✝✝✝✝

*Washington, D.C.
to the Dominican Republic*

I started to transcribe my log in the warm, sunny surroundings of
the Dominican Republic. It's hard to believe that only a few weeks
earlier I had shoveled several inches of snow off the deck and
broken up the ice around *Sabra*'s slip on the Potomac River. Here in
the Caribbean the temperature hardly varies more than a few degrees
from a perfect 77° F. I had almost forgotten the bitter cold on the trip
down the Potomac River, Chesapeake Bay, and along the Intracoastal
Waterway (ICW) from Norfolk, Virginia to Beaufort, North Carolina. It was a penetrating cold that can only be felt on the water. No
amount of layers, sweaters, windbreakers, or parkas could keep it out.
Even hot coffee was only a very temporary relief as we huddled in
foul weather gear behind the dodger.

The painful cold of the winter sailing trip amidst the snow and
ice had its own special beauty—a crisp, clear air that made for wonderful pictures along the river and the waterway. In spite of the cold, my
friend Ellison and I were relishing this rare opportunity to sail in
midwinter when most of the boaters in this area are hauled out or
frozen in. We were also glad to be escaping after two of the worst
snowstorms in recent years had hit Washington, D.C. We didn't
realize it at the time, but we luckily missed a third major snowstorm.

The weather in Washington, D.C. is definitely for the ducks.

This was the first leg of a marine conservation voyage that would take us more than 5,000 miles to 22 sunny Caribbean islands. The voyage aboard *Sabra,* a Chinese junk-rigged schooner, was coordinated by the Center for Marine Conserevation in Washington, D.C. to observe and report on several marine conservation subjects including: plastic pollution in the ocean; exploitation of several species of endangered sea turtles; management of a newly designated humpback whale sanctuary; illegal trade in endangered species products such as tortoise-shell and black coral; and a unique opportunity to visit Cuba, the largest of the Caribbean islands, to learn more of Cuban environmental conservation activities.

The voyage was going to cap my two-year tenure as chairman of the Center and highlight the Center's interest in the Caribbean marine environment. The growth in tourism and related development investments there are viewed as major threats to the sensitive marine environment.

THE FIRST LEG

The marina operator thought we were crazy when we asked for help to break up the ice around *Sabra*'s slip so that we could safely motor out into the Potomac River. Shaking his head at these crazy

Ice is broken up behind *Sabra*'s pier on the Potomac River so that we can escape the Washington, D.C. winter and sail for the Caribbean.

yachties, he ordered one of the yard hands to run up and down the channel with an outboard skiff to clear a path in the ice. While the path was being cleared, I was struggling to wake up the cold engine and stiff transmission. As the starter motor ground away, I was thinking that very soon we would be in warmer climes where a touch of the starter brings the engine to life.

The trip down the Potomac River had a eerie quality to it because of the winter stillness and the feeling of emptiness. Normally the river is a buzz of activity, but now everything around it seemed to be in deep hibernation. We spent a good deal of time on the lookout for thin sheets of ice that were floating on or just below the surface. We knew the ice was there because we could see a few birds seemingly walking on water. We were worried that a large sheet of ice, even a fraction of an inch thick, would have enough inertia to do a lot of damage to a thin fiberglass hull in a head-on collision. There was no point in starting a long voyage with a deep gouge in the hull, or worse yet, a hole.

We reached the mouth of the Potomac and Chesapeake Bay at night. The wind and sea state had picked up considerably at the mouth of the river but we decided against looking for a protected anchorage. We were determined to push southward as fast as possible towards warmer weather. After all, we were about to embark on a midwinter ocean voyage; a little chop on the bay wasn't going to make us scurry for cover.

However, as an added precaution we turned on our new toy—a satellite navigation receiver and computer (SatNav). Normally, Chesapeake Bay cruising doesn't require much more than eyeball navigation with an occasional reference to a compass and an eye on the depth sounder. But I was eager to experiment with this electronic wonder, which later proved to be so useful in finding the Caribbean. I was also eager to make the fastest possible passage and anxious about mishaps in this extremely cold water.

All night we motored against cold headwinds past familiar flashers—6-second Sharps Island, 10-second Point No Point, 15-second Wolf Trap . . . We fortified ourselves with coffee and hot chocolate and stared with amazement at the unerring SatNav readouts. By morning, Norfolk and the promise of a hot shower were within eyesight.

Next came the Intracoastal Waterway, more commonly referred to as the ICW or the "ditch." Norfolk is at mile zero of the ICW and our intermediate destination of Beaufort, North Carolina was a couple

A cold, crisp sunset on the Potomac River.

of hundred miles further south, and we hoped more than a few degrees warmer. About 50 miles south of Norfolk we found ourselves stuck in Coinjock, North Carolina, a popular two-gas-station "intersection" along the ICW. We were stalled for two days while a gale blew itself out on Albemarle Sound, further south. When the weather improved, we made a mad dash for Beaufort to resume our scheduled departure from the U.S. mainland by February 13. Our concern with the schedule was brought on by a need to meet with the humpback whales at their Dominican Republic wintering grounds before they started the annual migration north around the first of March.

One of my boating friends, on hearing that we were stuck in

Winter's stillness along the Intracoastal Waterway.

Coinjock, told me that the Coinjockians always order up bad weather on the sound. It strands boaters and that's good for the local economy. Actually, this was the second time I had been forced to extend my visit in Coinjock beyond a quick refueling stopover. I was thinking about buying property and running for office.

Ellison departed at Beaufort and my brother joined me for the offshore passage to the Dominican Republic. It had briefly crossed my mind that February 13, our departure date, was a Friday. But not being a superstitious person, I paid the coincidence no heed. Three hours out of the Beaufort Inlet and under power in an unusually calm Atlantic, the diesel engine quit with serious problems. There was oil all over the engine box and the engine was making a horrible metal-on-metal clanking noise. Apparently a piece of the head had broken on one cylinder and the valve stems were banging into the loose rocker arm assembly. Friday the 13th took on a new meaning and I promptly apologized to the gods.

We sailed very slowly back to the inlet and then over the VHF radio called for a tow to the Spooners Creek Yacht Marina where we awaited the diesel mechanic and the necessary engine parts. We were delayed at the marina for three days due to the weekend and a severe ice storm in North Carolina, which prevented the mechanic from reaching us.

The annoyance and frustration of the delay were somewhat softened by the warm welcome and the unusual hobby of the marina owner and his son. Paul, the son, was constructing a huge electronic pipe organ in a 20-foot-high addition to the marina chandlery. The organ has 15 ranks of pipes (938 pipes in all) ranging from a fraction of an inch in diameter and less than an inch tall to a foot in diameter and 17 feet tall. All the pipes were acquired from church sales or demolitions. Paul added a modern electronic keyboard, which controls the compressed air to these pipes. Bruce, his father, plays the organ for his amusement and the pleasure of marina visitors. His specialty is popular show tunes. The whole scene was surrealistic—an enormous pipe organ in a chandlery and melodious show tunes drifting over an icebound marina.

Another incident at Spooners Creek made us aware of how differently the world behaves outside of the hectic, what-have-you-done-for-me-lately, metropolitan areas and how refreshing it is to encounter these differences in a slow-paced boat cruise. Bruce was having difficulty loading an updated accounting software package into his computer. The problem played itself right into my brother's strong suit, and after a few minutes Raf had the problem licked. Bruce thanked him for the assistance and that was that. Raf wondered if the man knew exactly how valuable a consulting service he had just received free of charge. But later, when Bruce let us use his extensively equipped woodworking shop for some minor boat repairs, we realized that people around here are just naturally friendly and help is freely given to strangers without much concern for its monetary value.

Friday the 13th defeats our first attempt to leave the mainland.
We're towed back to North Carolina.

THE GULF STREAM

For three days prior to our second departure from the U.S. main-land, while waiting for the engine repairs, we carefully monitored our satellite navigation unit to be sure we understood its inner workings and had a complete schedule of upcoming satellite contacts. I was truly amazed by this electronic genie. Only $9'' \times 6'' \times 4''$, this little box does more than a room full of computers did just 25 years ago when

Before we slip into our bathing suits we must endure the cold North Atlantic.

THE GULF STREAM

The Gulf Stream is an immense natural phenomenon that goes unnoticed by almost everyone, even those people who live on the mid-Atlantic and southeastern coast of the U.S. within tens of miles of this gargantuan saltwater river. About 70 miles off the coast of North Carolina, the Gulf Stream has a volume of 70 million cubic meters per second, or 3,500 times greater than the flow of the Mississippi. In volume, the Gulf Stream is larger than all the fresh water rivers in the world put together.

The Gulf Stream starts as the Equatorial Current moving from east to west under the force of the easterly trades in the tropical Atlantic. South America deflects the current northward and it rushes into the Caribbean through gaps formed by the Caribbean islands. A small portion of the current, called the Antilles Current, does not enter the Caribbean but flows instead along Puerto Rico and Cuba's north coasts towards Florida. The larger portion of the Equatorial Current circles the Gulf of Mexico and exits between Cuba and Florida to meet the Antilles Current, thus forming the Gulf Stream. The Stream then flows in a northeasterly direction eventually turning easterly across the Atlantic where it again divides with a portion moving northward along the Norwegian coast and another portion moving southward towards the origins of the Equatorial Current.

To a sailor and other small-boat operators, the Gulf Stream is very noticeable, with a distinct temperature and color difference from the surrounding seas. But an even more noticeable feature is the effect of the stream's 1- to 4-knot flow in helping or hindering one's progress. When the current flow is opposite to the wind's direction, the Gulf Stream is at its most noticeable and the crew is generally so seasick that all they can think about is getting out of it.

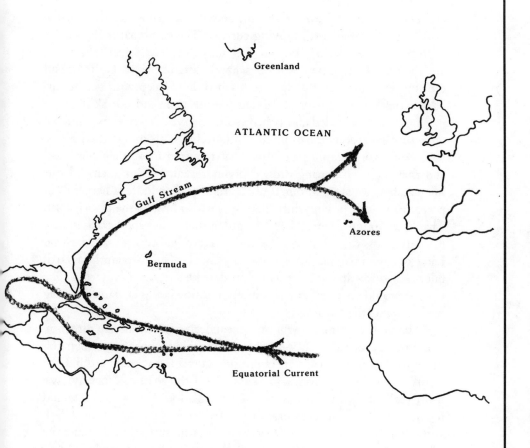

I started working in the aerospace industry. With the help of six Navy satellites in polar orbit around the earth, it computes our position to within a few hundred yards and tells us the "exact" time to atomic clock accuracy. In addition to being awed by this gadget, I was delighted to finally make some practical use of all that military hardware I've paid for all these years with my taxes.

Within a day out of Beaufort Inlet we ran into the Gulf Stream, and encountered a "war" going on between a strong wind from the north and a sizable north flowing current. The combination is deadly, with huge, irregular breaking waves, maybe 15 or 20 feet tall. There are plenty of published warnings about attempting a Gulf Stream crossing in a norther. But we had a schedule to keep with the humpback whales and we were confident of the boat and our skills.

Sabra was pounded and lashed from one wave to the next, and we were thrown around the cabin like billiard balls caroming off cushions. You could forget doing anything that required more than one hand and that included getting dressed or undressed. During many of our off watches, we slept in our foul weather gear and safety harnesses in preparation for our next shift. Eating was also low on the priority list. Thanks to granola bars, M & Ms, gingersnaps, and soda crackers, we made it across the 50-mile wide Gulf Stream before we wasted away. Later on, we imagined that a few days in the Gulf Stream in a small but luxuriously appointed yacht would make a terrific "fat farm." The weight would come off and absolutely nothing could be gained during one's stay in the stream.

The Gulf Stream, flowing in a meandering northeasterly direction along the Carolina coast, is capable of sweeping a boat more than 100 miles in a day. It is truly an impressive current that starts around the straits of Florida and eventually ends up off the coast of Norway. We had excellent information as to the stream's location on the date and intended path of our crossing, thanks to oceanographer Jenifer Clark at the National Oceanic and Atmospheric Administration. Because the stream is considerably warmer than the surrounding water, NOAA is able to pinpoint its location precisely, using daily remote temperature sensing from satellites.

Jenifer was eager to have us measure the water temperature along our course as surface truth data to compare with her satellite data. We started to keep an hourly temperature log along with our satellite position fixes, but after several measurements the thermometer broke in the heavy seas. Later I read about a good trick to avoid damaging

the thermometer on the hull in heavy seas. You simply pump fresh
seawater into the toilet bowl and measure its temperature in the safety
of the head. (See the appendix for more on the Gulf Stream.)

We knew we were out of the Gulf Stream when the waves became
more regular and less intimidating. We were just starting to get used
to the rough seas. It's like becoming accustomed to driving fast on the
interstate highways after doing it for hours. However, the respite was
short-lived as we were hit by two successive gales (or near gales), each
lasting a day and a half. Between gales we had equally annoying calms
which mean absolutely no progress toward the longed-for warm trade
winds, just a lot of uncomfortable wallowing.

We measure distance southward by the slow, slow rise of the
thermometer.

Fortunately, the junk rig really comes into its own when frequent sail changes are required. The main and foresail are fully battened sails that raise and lower like venetian blinds. There is no need to wrestle with flogging jibs or to tie off reefed mains. The lazyjacks and battens keep everything quietly under control and all sail changes can be made from the cockpit with no anxious moments on the slippery and bouncy foredeck. (See the appendix for more on the junk rig.)

During one calm, we spotted a pod of whales which we thought to be sei whales from their above water profiles and diving patterns. They didn't get any closesr to us than about 100 yards. Maybe they didn't like the Harry Chapin album we were playing at the time. We planned to be more selective with music next time we encounter whales.

THE SARGASSO SEA

The Sargasso Sea stretches roughly from just north of Bermuda to Puerto Rico, and is bounded by the Gulf Stream on the west and the Azores on the east. It is the only named sea not bordered by land masses. Rather, it is identified by its distinctive characteristics. The water in the sea contains sargassum weed and is very salty and exceptionally clear and clean, due to a lack of sediments running off land and the tiny floating plants and animals so prevalent near shorelines. Since the time of Columbus, stories have persisted of huge beds of floating weeds thick enough to trap a vessel and carry it endlessly around the circular currents of the Sargasso. We saw quite a bit of the sargassum plant, but none of it in more than two-foot-square patches. We picked up some of it but were unable to detect any life with the unaided eye other than the weed itself and the gas bubbles that keep it afloat. The sargassum forms an important habitat for a number of fish and it is thought to be a feeding area for young sea turtles. (See the appendix for more on the Sargasso Sea.)

Because of the nearly closed circulation patterns of the Sargasso Sea, I attempted to conduct a pollution count of visible plastic debris. According to the Department of Commerce, this is done by making 20-minute observations ahead and to the right and left of the boat's

Investigating the mystery of sargassum weed in the Sargasso Sea.

course, noting with the unaided eye all forms of foreign matter. I stared for hours at a time at the ocean with its beautiful electric blue colorations and constantly shifting shapes. It was like staring at flames in a fireplace or clouds drifting overhead. It was mesmerizing. But I didn't find much in the way of visible plastic.

In the more than 1,000 miles from Beaufort to the Dominican Republic, I identified and recorded the following floating foreign matter: one piece of lumber approximately $1'' \times 6'' \times 3'$; one wine bottle of unknown vintage; one Ragu spaghetti sauce bottle; one eight-inch diameter Styrofoam sphere; an orange two-gallon plastic

SARGASSO SEA

The mere mention of the Sargasso Sea conjures up a mental picture of mythical sea monsters and legendary square-riggers perpetually stuck in huge masses of weeds aimlessly and forever drifting under a scorching sun. From the time of Columbus we have had a mixture of tall tales and science regarding the mysteries of sargassum weed and the Sargasso Sea. In modern times, the "Devil's Triangle," in the southwest corner of the Sargasso, has contributed to the doomed-water reputation of this Sea.

The Sargasso Sea, named by the Portuguese for the grapelike appearance of sargassum weed, lies roughly between Greenland, the Azores, Cuba, and the continental shelf of the U.S. It is the only sea on earth that is bordered by water rather than land masses. It is the Atlantic's deepest mid-waters and a virtual desert sea. The lack of nutrients in waters so far from coastlines makes the sea a watery desert and contribute to its vivid, electric blue color.

Although sargassum weed is no longer as profuse as it was in Columbus' time, when his crew thought the weed beds were islands, it is still one of the major features of the Sargasso. Some define the borders of the sea by the existence of this weed.

As a result of the Antilles current to the south and the Gulf Stream to the west and north, the Sargasso has an encirculating motion which is thought to entrap pollutants in this remote body of water. Air-transported dust containing land-based pollutants drifts over the Sargasso and contributes to the insidious burden of pollution, especially the more exotic materials such as DDT and PCB. Plastic debris from commercial shipping and tar balls from oil spillage, pumping of bilges, cleaning of oil tanks, and ballasting losses help to keep the Sargasso well supplied with man's wastes.

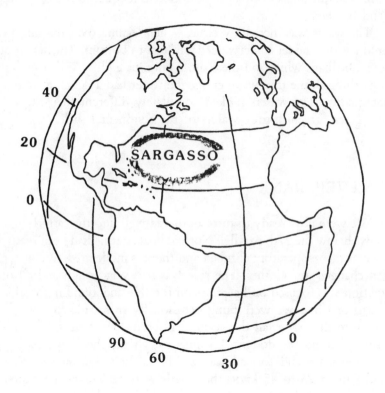

jug, a 6″ × 18″ × 4″ unidentified piece of plastic; and a few strips of plastic garbage bag three to four inches long.

Considering that billions of pounds of garbage are dumped in the ocean each year, I was somewhat surprised to encounter so little visible pollution on a 1,000-mile track. But scientists speculate that the Sargasso may actually rid itself of floating debris by collecting it and then sinking it, acting like a huge circulating bathtub drain. The cleanliness and clarity of the Sargasso was misleading. Later on this trip I would realize the full impact of plastic pollution as it concentrates on remote island beaches.

The water was incredibly clear. When leaning over the rail, you could see the rudder underwater from top to bottom. The whitecaps were a brilliant white and the foam a pure, pale blue. When sunlight shone through the thin wave crests, the water had a delicious translucent quality. The waters looked completely different than the sediment-laden, greenish-grey waters of the continental shelf.

SILVER BANK

We were now ready to turn south and well into the easterly trade windw below the 27th parallel. Normal boat routine had been reestablished as the temperature climbed and the seas moderated. We ate and even changed our clothes. The ride was still very rough and all our attention was focused on keeping comfortable and avoiding breaking an arm or rib as we were flung occasionally from side to side.

Up to this point, all the sailing had been done from the huddled position behind the dodger. Fortunately, all the sheets and halyards from the main and foresail lead to the cockpit. During the heavy winds, about 25 to 45 knots, both sails were reefed to one exposed panel. But now that the steady easterly trades were beginning to assert themselves, the sails were fully exposed and *Sabra*'s junk rig did what it does best—sail off the wind. And we were able to shake off our foul weather gear and enjoy the entire deck.

About 75 miles northeast of the Dominican Republic is a shoal known as Silver Bank. This is one of the major winter breeding grounds of the humpback whales that summer in the northeast in such areas as Stellwagen Bank off Cape Cod. Not a bad life for a whale.

With a great deal of support from the Center, local environmental groups persuaded the Dominican government to declare Silver Bank a humpback whale sanctuary. This means no dumping in the area, no drilling for gas or oil, no killing of marine mammals, no commercial vessels during the breeding season, and no dredging or seabed alterations. Most importantly, it focuses public attention on the endangered humpback whale and promotes its protection. (See the appendix for more or marine sanctuaries.)

We had arrived in time. The pain of a winter crossing had paid off for many whales had not yet started their northward migration. As we approached this area, we saw several whale blows off in the distance. At several hundred yards it's hard to make out a shape but as soon as we saw the whales breaching, jumping completely out of the water, we were sure they were humpbacks. They didn't come any closer, even though Harry Chapin had by now been replaced by the incesssant beat of Caribbean FM radio music. We were now into heavy reggae and salsa.

Around dusk, a solitary whale started to head our way. Every few minutes it would roll on its side exposing an enormous winglike fin. It looked as if it were waving at us as it approached closer and closer. At about 30 feet, its huge fluke came out of the water and then the immense body slid within 10 feet of the boat! We could have touched it with a boat hook. It was much too dark by then to photograph the animal, but the image of this 30- to 50-ton animal gently gliding past our fragile five-ton boat was indelibly recorded in our minds.

Following that spectacular encounter with the humpback, we made a course straight for Puerto Plata, hoping to reach the harbor with first light and plenty of time to go through customs and immigration formalities. This was to be my first foreign port and I wanted to be ready for all those horror stories I had read about customs procedures.

We spotted Mt. Isabella de Torres, a natural signpost for Puerto Plata, and hoisted the yellow Q flag in preparation for our entry into the harbor.

HUMPBACK WHALES
AND THE SILVER BANK SANCTUARY

By the late 1800s, whalers had turned their attention to the slow-moving humpbacks, as the favored right and bowhead whales were depleted. Less than a century later, when humpbacks finally received international protection from commercial whaling, their worldwide population had been reduced from an estimated 100,000 to about 15,000. Today there are two major populations, one in the north Atlantic estimated at about 6,000 to 8,000 animals, and one in the north Pacific, estimated at about 2,000 animals.

Humpbacks undertake long migrations each year from their northern summer feeding grounds to the warm tropical waters in which they mate and bear their calves. In the North Pacific, humpbacks summer off Alaska and migrate south to Hawaii or to waters off Mexico. In the North Atlantic, humpbacks spend the summer in three separate areas: Greenland, Newfoundland-Labrador, and Nova Scotia-Gulf of Maine. Whales from these three populations migrate south to the Caribbean for the winter. The major wintering ground in the Caribbean is Silver Bank, a shallow 650-square-mile bank about 70 miles north of the Dominican Republic. Researchers have estimated that up to 3,500 whales may be present on Silver Bank at peak times of the year.

Humpbacks are considered the most playful of the large whales. They can often be seen slapping the water with their large flippers, and breaching—thrusting themselves out of the water and landing with a resounding crash.

Humpback males are also famous for their haunting songs, perhaps the longest and most complex of any song in the animal kingdom. Although the precise function of the songs is debated, they are believed to be associated with courtship. Curiously, in spite of intensive research on the breeding grounds, neither mating nor calving has ever been observed.

In 1986, Joaquin Balaguer, the newly elected president of the Dominican Republic, designated Silver Bank as a sanctuary for humpback whales. The sanctuary designation forbids the hunting, capturing, or injuring of any marine mammals. It also forbids the discharging or deposition of contaminated, explosive, or electrical materials. Finally, the designation prohibits dredging, drilling, or any alteration of the sea bottom or construction on the bank. Most importantly, the designation of the sanctuary creates a focus for additional research of the humpback whale population.

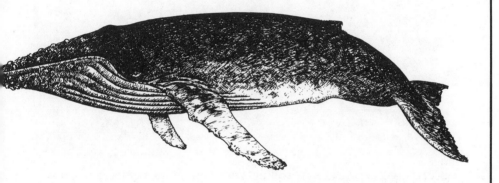

Our first experience at hauling up a yellow quarantine flag prior
to entering a foreign port—Puerto Plata, Dominican Republic.

PUERTO PLATA, DOMINICAN REPUBLIC

The harbor itself proved to be a difficult and unattractive anchorage. It was open to ocean swells, directly under the plume of an
uncontrolled power plant smoke stack, and in line with the town's
untreated sewage outfall. To make matters worse, the dinghy dock was
an old, rundown concrete pier, which required quite a bit of scrambling to get ashore.

As we were dropping anchor, a nearby boat called us on the VHF
radio to welcome us and in the same breath tell us that this was the

worst place they had ever been. We weren't exactly cheered by this reception, but we completed the anchoring drill and awaited customs in response to the quarantine flag.

Customs came in the form of four men in a very, very small dinghy. One was uniformed and armed and the other three looked like stevedores. They boarded and proceeded to ask lots of expected questions and to search the boat. They showed particular interest in my tool kit and Raf's Chapstick. We never could understand their interest in these items. They were very friendly and after some fumbling over what we owed them, considering that this was Saturday and overtime, we finally received our clearance and hoisted the Dominican Republic courtesy flag. We were told that in this country you have to clear customs from port to port, so we planned to see them again on our way to Samana in the next few days. As they left, I gave each of them a Center for Marine Conservation frisbee with the humpback logo. They were delighted with the gift. Our last sight of them was of four

First impressions of the Caribbean paradise include a belching smokestack and a rickety, run-down pier.

big men in a rub-a-dub-tub of a dinghy rowing ashore and waving their new frisbees.

At the dock we met the "boat boys" who act as guides and procurers for anything arriving sailors might want. As we would learn later, boat boys do this at "yachty" prices, which are many times what things cost in the normal local economy. For example, they handled my first and last load of laundry, one pillowcase full, for $31! By contrast, a complete pizza dinner and drink ashore costs $2.50, an airmail letter to the U.S. costs nine cents, and the bus to anywhere in the area costs eight cents.

Dominican Republic customs and immigration officials depart, showing off the "Save the Whales" Frisbees we gave them.

Everyone we met in Puerto Plata was extremely friendly and helpful. I needed a special resistor for my ailing alternator and the local electric parts dealer handed me a big box of junk parts and his ohm meter with which to sort through his collection of unmarked resistors. I sat on his stoop for about an hour and finally found the right part.

My brother flew back to Boston and while I awaited my son Scott's arrival for the next leg of the trip, I wandered in and out of the tourist shops in search of tortoiseshell and black coral jewelry. Sea turtles and black coral are species protected by the Convention on International Trade in Endangered Species of Wild Fauna and Flora (CITES). For the 95 nations which are CITES members, international trade in sea turtle products is prohibited, and trade in black coral is regulated to avoid further danger to the threatened species. The Dominican Republic is a member of this international convention. (See the appendix for more on threatened sea turtles.)

I didn't have to search for stores selling black coral and tortoiseshell. Actually, it would have been much harder to find a store that didn't carry these items. I didn't see how the Dominican government was going to curb international trade in these products because it appeared to be a mainstay in the tourist business of Puerto Plata. Every day, a cruise ship disgorged 1,000 tourists who hungrily foraged like locusts through the town's shops. In this poor economy, where a typical hotel employee earns $900 a year, asking the citizens to stop selling black coral would have been unthinkable.

In my own mind, I wondered whether there weren't environmental problems of higher priority for these people than the threat of black coral extinction. The uncovered sewer, open, burning dumps, uncontrolled smoke stack emissions, and filth in the streets came to mind much sooner than the extinction of black coral.

In the U.S., where we take basic environmental regulation of sewage, smokestack emissions, and solid waste disposal for granted, it is easy to forget more immediate environmental concerns. In the Dominican Republic, earning a living and basic public health are much more important and immediate problems.

I discovered a nonprofit development organization next to the wharf where youngsters were being trained as artisans. A major focus of this training is jewelry making, specifically black coral jewelry. Private funds were being raised for this foundation to get kids off the streets and give them useful jobs.

As long as tourists demand the black coral jewelry, black coral

Local artisans are encouraged to produce jewelry from endangered species products.

jewelry making will be treated as an important source of employment and income. Rather than preaching to local artisans, the message concerning the threat to black coral should be aimed at the tourists. Notices on cruise ships, airplanes and airports, and hotels could raise awareness and help curb the market for endangered species products. Then and only then would local artisans redirect their handicraft efforts to other, less damaging tourist products.

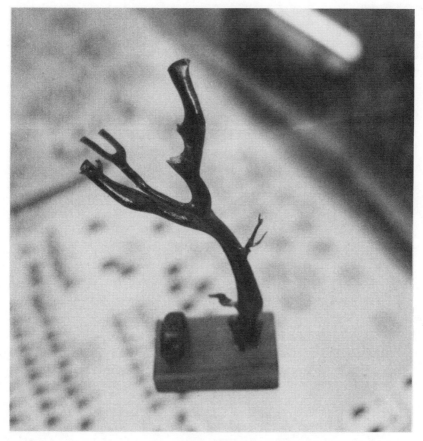

Endangered species products like this black coral sculpture are
freely sold in the Dominican Republic and all over the Caribbean.

Black coral necklaces.

SANTA BARBARA DE SAMANA

Before leaving Puerto Plata, I had an opportunity to appear before a high school assembly to say a few words of thanks for the Dominican government's foresight in declaring Silver Bank a humpback whale sanctuary. The night before departing, the mayor of Puerto Plata, in a brief ceremony at the town plaza, presented me with a distinguished visitor citation while the kids paraded around the plaza carrying "Flo," a 35-foot balloon whale that the Center had sent for the occasion.

The trip to Samana Bay, at the eastern end of the Dominican

Republic, was an uncomfortable windward slog under sail and power. We spent 30 hours bashing our way eastward against the trades. William F. Buckley Jr. is quoted as saying that "gentlemen never go to windward." I appreciate that sentiment even more now.

During the trip, a ⅜-inch stainless steel shackle broke, letting go the foresail and giving some indication of the rough ride. Scott needed no such evidence as he lay almost comatose for the entire 30 hours as a result of severe seasickness. He didn't have this kind of sailing in mind when he joined the project in the sunny Caribbean. But I kept assuring

The mayor of Puerto Plata makes me an "honored visitor" for the Center's work with the Silver Bank humpback whale sanctuary. Photo by Scott Frankel.

I'm flanked by the chief of police and the mayor during the festivities honoring our visit. Photo by Scott Frankel.

Scott that as soon as we "turned the corner" and headed in a more southeasterly direction, we would be treated to the exhilaration of Caribbean trade wind sailing.

The town of Santa Barbara de Samana is a picturesque anchorage with a very small settlement in what the government wants to promote as a major tourist area. The bay itself is a staging area of sorts for humpback whales as they congregate for their annual migration north. As we sailed into the bay, we spotted several blows but never got close enough to see the whales.

I talked to a Canadian couple at a local hotel who told me of the wonderful whale watching opportunities that exist in the bay. Furthermore, they said that unlike Canada and the U.S., the Dominican Republic enforces no whale watching guidelines and thus you may motor right into a pod of whales! This kind of harassment of an endangered species is exactly what the Center wants to prevent while at the same time encouraging a whale watching industry. The Center for Marine Conservation supports local environmental groups, now that the sanctuary is established, to ensure that the area is well managed and continues to focus attention on the protection of these magnificent mammals.

Samana is a perfect area from which to promote whale watching for tourists, but I wonder how many Dominicans will come to partake in this activity. The local economy didn't look like it indulged environmental awareness. But there was plenty of evidence that the town was attempting to beautify the harbor area for tourists. Quite a bit of landscaping was being done on the waterfront and the beach area was relatively clean.

However, something has to be done about the untreated sewage

Puerto Plata children parade Flo, the Center's inflatable whale, around the town square.

which flows into the harbor. A few more hotels and more accessible connections to airports in Santo Domingo and Puerto Plata could help set the stage for a profitable whale watching industry along with an opportunity to conduct whale research in these winter breeding grounds. There is a real opportunity to help the Dominicans in the business and environmental planning of a whale watching industry similar to those in California and New England. There is also an opportunity to provide the technical guidance for establishing a research station at Samana Bay. This would complement New England studies of these gentle giants at both ends of their migratory route.

During our brief stay in Samana we replaced *Sabra*'s sails. The crossing to the Dominican Republic and our first bashing into the trades had been too much for the 10-year-old sails. Fortunately, we had ordered a new suit of tanbark sails before leaving on this adventure. In addition to replacing the frayed sails, I was also eager to see *Sabra* in the tanbark color which was more in character with the grass mat sails of the original Chinese junk.

Many Ways to Shower

✝✝✝✝✝

Puerto Rico to the Virgin Islands

abra departed Samana Bay and the Dominican Republic, headed eastward for the American territories of Puerto Rico and the Virgin Islands. Exactly 495 years and two months earlier, Columbus had departed Samana Bay on his homeward journey to Spain after his momentous discovery of the new World. Our departure was far less historic but it felt good to realize that we both depended on the winds for a safe and speedy journey.

On our way out of Samana Bay we also took a closer look at a small inlet called Bay of Arrows near the mouth of Samana Bay. This was where, on his second visit to the New World, Columbus built a fort to defend his men from the Caribe Indians. There is still some question as to his exact landfall on his first visit to the New World in 1492. Researchers from the National Geographic Society have been using computer simulations of wind and current patterns with transcripts of Columbus's original log to pinpoint his exact landfall in the Bahamas. But there is no question as to the location of his many landfalls during the second trip. The ruins of the fort are still here. The landing site we saw off *Sabra*'s deck must have looked remarkably similar to what Columbus saw almost 500 years ago. With the exception of a few corrugated metal rooftops here and there and the lack of "fierce Caribes," nothing much has changed in five centuries. It was like stepping into a time warp.

We were fortunate not only to have a brisk northeasterly wind on our beam but also to see several more humpback whales near the mouth of the bay. March through April is the time for the annual humpback migration to the northern waters of the Atlantic including New England and the Cape Cod region. Some researchers have suggested that the whales may congregate at Samana Bay just prior to their northward trek. Although our sighting didn't include the spectacular breaching performances we had seen earlier in the Silver Bank area, it was nonetheless a wonderful send-off and a last reminder of the importance of the Dominican Republic's newly designated Humpback Sanctuary at Silver Bank.

MAYAGUEZ AND PUERTO REAL, PUERTO RICO

The 140-mile crossing of the Mona Passage between Hispaniola and the west coast of Puerto Rico is reported to be a boisterous stretch of water. After our midwinter Gulf Stream adventure off North Carolina and the winter gales that followed en route to the Dominican Republic, this passage turned out to be a piece of cake, except for those who get seasick, as Scott did.

We were headed for Mayaguez, a commercial port and the customs entry point for the U.S. Thanks to our straightforward dead reckoning and the unmistakable landmark of 700-foot-tall Desecheo Island, part of the U.S. Caribbean National Wildlife Refuge, we fetched Mayaguez easily in the early hours of the morning.

Mayaguez is not exactly a picture-postcard harbor. It is a commercial port with a very odorous fish-processing plant nearby. We tied up at the wharf with no intention of staying longer than it would take to clear customs and do a bit of grocery shopping. For American citizens with a U.S.-documented pleasure vessel, the clearance process can be done over the telephone in a few minutes, a welcome contrast to the bureaucracy of the Dominican Republic's customs procedure. The shopping was also very convenient because we found all the familiar brands on our list of basic foodstuffs: Almost Home cookies, Skippy peanut butter, Wyler's lemonade, Dinty Moore stew, Nature Brand granola, M&Ms, etc.

Another reason for stopping at Mayaguez was to contact the Puerto Rican Department of Natural Resources (DNR) regarding a visit to Mona Island in the southern portion of the Mona Passage. This island is operated as a nature preserve and has been designated as critical nesting and foraging habitat for endangered sea turtles. It has both nesting beaches for endangered sea turtles and important coral reefs. The Center for Marine Conservation has a particular interest in this uninhabited island, which is about 50 miles southwest of Mayaguez.

Mona Island came to our attention early in 1985 when a 330-foot passenger ship en route from Mayaguez to the Dominican Republic ran aground on the coral reef surrounding the island and was abandoned by the owners after some unsuccessful salvage attempts. The wreck posed several environmental threats, including the discharge of oil and other hazardous fluids on the coral and nesting beach areas; the physical breakup of the coral as the hull grated against the reef; the deposition of harmful sediments resulting from the constant grinding action against the bottom; and the scattering of litter from the boat onto the beach, which also interferes with sea turtle nesting and the hatchlings' progress to the water. The DNR had already documented a decline in sea turtle nesting occurrence since the vessel's grounding.

The Center had been pressuring various federal agencies responsible for keeping our nation's waters clean and protecting endangered species to remove the wreck. It was clear that the owners had no intention of salvaging the wreck. Both the U.S. Army Corps of Engineers and the U.S. Coast Guard have taken refuge behind some ambiguous interpretations of the Clean Water Act and the Endangered Species Act to avoid having to spend the $1 million to $2 million estimated to remove the wreck. It was already too late to remove the vessel as the heavy winter swells pounded away at the hull, breaking it up and making salvaging more and more difficult. The heavy surf during the winter months had also made it impossible for *Sabra* to sail close to the site of the wreck and explore the damage.

The vessel was never removed and it is now up to Mother Nature to ever so slowly reclaim the beach.

From Mayaguez we continued southward along Puerto Rico's west coast to Puerto Real, a small fishing and seaside resort. With *Sabra*

ON THE SUBJECT OF SEASICKNESS:
I AM A VULCAN

by Scott Frankel

Crossing the Mona Passage was not as bad as we had expected. The 140-mile stretch of water between the Dominican Republic and Puerto Rico, which serves as one of the principal entrances to the Caribbean Sea, has a duly earned reputation for heavy summertime squalls, high seas, and confusing tidal currents. For our crossing however, the skies were clear and the ubiquitous easterly trades had a gracious and unusual northerly component, allowing us to fetch Puerto Rico's western shore in a brisk sail.

After setting up Pierre, the windvane navigator, and noting our course on the compass, there wasn't much to do except hold on as we bucked and rolled with the seas. We had set out early on a typically warm and sunny Caribbean morning. The day was spent watching the boat tackle wave after wave in its upwind climb towards Mayaguez.

It wasn't until late afternoon that I became seasick. With another 15 to 20 hours of sailing still ahead of us, I realized that if I didn't do something to counter the apparent misinformation between my brain and middle ear, I'd go comatose again, and that'd be the end of my pleasure cruise across the Mona Passage. What could I do? I looked at the horizon and my thoughts wandered. I began replaying "Star Trek" episodes in my mind, paying close attention to the one where Mr. Spock gets attacked by the single-celled plastic vomit creature on the planet Denova. The creature's sting, being particularly painful, required of Spock all of his physical and ethnic strength to remain composed. He reminded himself and the viewing audience that pain is a thing of the mind.

Being a Vulcan, his mind was almost completely subject to his conscious will. Drawing to bear his mind in controlled concentration allowed him to regain his composure, return to his duties, and carry himself with the stoic efficiency befitting a Vulcan.

I tried it. "I am a Vulcan," I said. "Seasickness is a thing of the mind and the mind can be controlled."

Soon I felt better. I watched the setting sun carve black hollows in the troughs of wavelets in front of us. As darkness began to settle, I could sense the perimeter of the horizon shrink a little bit, making the ocean seem warmer and more hospitable. I even thought the swells were getting shallower. Was I cured?

By nightfall, when it was really dark, I realized that relief had been temporary. The churning fullness of my empty stomach had returned, bringing with it a sense of dread for the impending moonlit sail eastward. Sustained by novelty, the Vulcan cure had proven no match against the relentless pitch and roll of the sea. Resigned, I put on the safety harness and fastened it to the lifeline. There was nothing left to do but lie down in the open cockpit and let the undulating velvet of the Caribbean fetch me some sleep.

PLASTIC POLLUTION

Since its invention more than 40 years ago, plastic has become such an integral part of life that it is difficult to survey one's surroundings without finding plastic items in use, and, unfortunately, in disuse. In the vast reaches of the ocean and remote, uninhabited beaches, plastic debris reminds us of our propensity to carelessly throw things away.

The durable characteristics that have made plastics so convenient for packaging, household products, and commercial equipment also make it a continuing, nondegradable, and persistent presence in the marine environment. Environmental impacts arise from entanglement of marine animals in plastic debris and from ingestion of plastics by marine organisms. Plastic debris can cause potential threats to humans when divers become entangled or vessels become fouled in debris. The depletion of fishery resources by discarded nets and aesthetic degradation resulting in lost tourist revenues or costly cleanup all contribute to significant economic impacts caused by plastic debris.

Sea turtles, sea lions, seals, and birds are commonly entangled in discarded fragments of fishing nets, plastic strapping bands used to bind containers, monofilament fishing line, and six-pack connectors used to carry beverage cans. Marine animals may also ingest plastic debris while feeding on other organisms or mistake plastic for authentic food items. Sea turtles mistake plastic bags and plastic sheeting for jellyfish, and many species of seabirds ingest plastic resin pellets (the raw form of plastic after it has been synthesized from petrochemicals).

Another major problem tied to plastic debris has been the issue of "ghost" fishing or the ability of lost or dicarded fishing nets to continue to catch fish indefinitely. Free-floating nets have been reported to catch large numbers of commercially valuable species of finfish and shellfish years after they have been lost.

Unfortunately, most of the information on plastic debris, such as the quantities or sources of plastic in the marine environment, is anecdotal. A synthesis of such information suggests that the biological and economic impacts may be significant. Even after the sources and impacts of plastic debris in the ocean are well documented, legal interpretation, enforcement problems, and the lack of public education have hampered the implementation of effective means to control the use and disposal of plastics in the marine environment.

tied up at the local fishing dock for the night, we partook of a well deserved "happy hour" in one of the outdoor cafes along the waterfront.

The windward bashing had temporarily abated; we were looking ahead to daysailing and no more overnight passages for quite some time. Going around the south coast of Puerto Rico also meant that we would be protected from any late winter northerlies. Apart from a broken shackle (and wear 'n' tear on the 10-year-old frayed sails that had been replaced in Samana Bay), *Sabra* and crew were doing just fine.

Sabra's burgee: "Tough on the outside, sweet on the inside."

The crew of one of the sailboats that we had previously met in Puerto Plata, again in Samana Bay, and again in Mayaguez, had warned us that Puerto Real was full of thieves, and we should bypass it in favor of Boqueron further south. We suspected this was probably nonsense coming from one person's singular experience and paid no attention to the warning. As it turned out, we had a pleasant time in Puerto Real and noted its cleanliness, New Orleans-style architecture, dockside hospitality, and friendly people. The admonition about thieves reminded me of my own unflattering stereotyping of Puerto Ricans based on some past business dealings with a Puerto Rican firm and several unpleasant New York City adventures. Later on our trip, we met a Puerto Rican bird researcher who told us that the islanders do not particularly like mainland Americans and especially not New York Puerto Ricans whom they refer to as "Newyoricans" speaking "Spanglish."

THE SOUTH COAST OF PUERTO RICO

Our next stop was Boqueron, where we fueled up, bought some ice, and mailed a few letters. Boqueron is another seaside resort with a lovely crescent beach and a very picturesque anchorage. However, we elected not to anchor for the night and instead headed for Parguera, a site that was proposed for, but failed to achieve, national marine sanctuary status. Parguera is a sportfishing village and weekend resort noted for its beautiful phosphorescent waters. The waters are inhabited by a type of plankton that illuminate the water when disturbed. Unfortunately, the effect is most noticeable on moonless nights, and we had a bright moon on the evening of our visit.

The coastline around Parguera is dotted with islands and many waterfront homes. The homes have one edge of their foundation on shore and the other on stilts in the water. I suspect many of the residents around the bay dump their sewage directly into the bay. But as long as strict controls can be maintained to prevent overdevelopment of the area, Parguera and the bay will continue to be very attractive and a valuable and unique marine resource.

From Parguera we headed for Ponce, the second largest city in

Puerto Rico and the home of the much-advertised Ponce Yacht and Fishing Club. We tied up at this elegant yacht club and for $16 were allowed to use their facilities for the night. To us that meant the all-important shower.

For those interested in the more mundane details of long distance cruising, let me describe the five kinds of showers we encountered on the voyage: (1) the one-handed cold sponge bath with the other hand holding onto the boat for dear life; (2) the jump in the ocean with a shampoo bottle (hard soap doesn't lather in salt water) followed by a very quick on-board freshwater rinse; (3) an extravagant on-board hot or cold shower using our precious freshwater supply; (4) a dockside hosing down using someone else's fresh water; and (5) an honest hot water shower in a marina. Hair suffers the most in the absence of fresh water or with limited freshwater rinses—it turns to straw. Therefore, when ashore, I always carried a small vial of shampoo with me in case I find a hotel or restaurant restroom with running water and non-spring-loaded faucets.

Unfortunately, for all its advertised renown, the Ponce Yacht and Fishing Club had outdoor shower stalls but no hot water. So we had a more elegant variation of a Number 4.

Following the shower, we hitched a ride into town and dined out to celebrate the skipper's 50th birthday. We stuffed ourselves on shrimp and plantains. Bloated on a good restaurant meal after weeks of our own attempts at cooking, we headed back to the boat. All the way back I kept thinking about a bumper sticker that read, "Age is unimportant unless you're a cheese."

On our way to Ponce, and for that matter all along the south coast of Puerto Rico, we saw what we thought were marker buoys for drift nets. The cruising guide for this region warns of Japanese tuna nets and the serious propeller damage that can result from running into one. We questioned several fisherman about these buoys and were told that they marked fish traps and not fishing nets. I hope they were fish traps, because drift nets are not only hazardous to boat propellers, they are also a major cause of entanglement for endangered sea turtles, sea birds, and marine mammals. The Center is fighting the use of drift nets in American coastal waters because of the indiscriminate deaths of endangered species caused by entanglement.

The next day, we left Ponce and headed for Salinas, another fishing and resort community and also a proposed marine sanctuary. As in Parguera, we found a lovely bay, a good anchorage, and very pleasant waterfront surroundings. There were a few shorefront homes and sport fishing piers in the main bay. We tied up to a small dock adjoining a restaurant and had our now daily one-beer "happy hour," as we sampled the local culture.

I tried to make a telephone call but by now I had accumulated sufficient data for another important environmental statistic: only one out of four public telephones in the Caribbean is in working order. A telephone repairman, whom I met later in the trip, told me that a big source of public telephone damage is caused by people using the many different national coins of the Caribbean. I'm guilty of this offense, having discovered that the 25-cent piece of the Dominican Republic, which is worth about seven cents, works in place of a U.S. quarter.

I haven't said anything about noise pollution on this trip because one man's noise can be another's music. For example, the high-pitched whine of motor scooters in the Dominican Republic was deafening. But then again, I love the deep, throbbing sound of a Harley Davidson. Here in the small bay of Salinas, as in other shoreline resorts, the music blared until the early morning hours. What made it worse is that the sound carried so well across the still water, and the competing beats all around the bay added up to one big unmistakable noise.

On our way from Salinas to Palmas del Mar, we saw an unusually dark and threatening storm brewing ahead of us. Since we were sailing close to many reefs, we decided to run for cover at a convenient oil refinery depot. It was a difficult place to anchor because of all the chain and anchor line needed to hold the boat in the 40- to 50-foot-deep water normally used to accommodate very deep draft tankers. But it felt safer than the coral reefs along the coast obscured by the sediment-rich waters.

I was surprised by how oil- and litter-free the water appeared in this small, confined industrial harbor. The beach area was also surprisingly free of litter and petrochemical debris and looked as good as any other recreational beach we had seen so far on this trip. No one would think of sailing with a gleaming white-hulled boat into a refinery depot on the U.S. Gulf of Mexico coast, unless in an extreme emergency. I think the cleanliness of these harbor waters and shoreline says something about the successful efforts that can be taken by industry and government to keep an obviously pollution-prone environment so clean.

We didn't stay long at the refinery because the storm passed harmlessly overhead and we didn't want to be caught in that small confined harbor when one of the tankers started to maneuver. We resumed our eastward sail to Palmas del Mar on the east coast of Puerto Rico.

PALMAS DEL MAR

Before crossing Vieques Sound to the island of Culebra, we stopped off at Palmas del Mar to prepare ourselves for the differences between a fully developed and polished resort and an uncut diamond in the rough.

Palmas del Mar is a newly built resort community that has to be seen firsthand to be appreciated. This 2,700-acre resort aspires to look like the French and Italian Rivieras with red-tiled roofs and white stucco buildings clinging to the hillsides and very expensive yachts in the harbor. The resort boasts of seven elegant restaurants, a golf course, 20 tennis courts, two hotels, a casino, a "wellness" center, miles of beaches, riding stables, sailing school, and numerous villas and town houses. There is also an overabundance of realty companies competing for your attention to buy or rent one of their condos, villas, or time-share units.

The grounds are beautifully landscaped, well manicured, and constantly patrolled by armed guards. The beaches are raked to keep them well groomed for the guests. The ambience reminded me of the old TV series "The Prisoner," starring Patrick McGoohan. We were only there a short while but I was already beginning to feel well taken care of like Number 6. We extended the stay only because the marina had a hot shower and Number 6 could luxuriate with a Number 5.

On our last day in this mega-resort, while lounging at the hotel over a cup of coffee, I gave in to the persistent sales pitches and pretended to be someone just in on his "yacht" and interested in real estate. We immediately received a personal tour of the resort complex with a close look at several $200,000 to $400,000 units. Unfortunately, none was currently available with a slip small enough for my "yacht," so I politely declined the opportunity to buy and went for an ice cream cone instead.

Palmas del Mar is a very comfortable setting if you bring lots of money and a desire to immerse yourself in a planned, overly neat, man-made environment. Don't go there to see the natural wildlife and scenery of the Caribbean.

CULEBRA

Due east of Puerto Rico and about halfway to St. Thomas is the small U.S. island of Culebra. This 7,000-acre island was settled by the Spanish following its discovery by Columbus on his second voyage. It was ceded to the U.S. following the Spanish-American War in 1901

Beautiful coral specimens washed up on a Culebra beach. Photo by Scott Frankel.

ENDANGERED SPECIES

Of the estimated five to 10 million species in the world today, approximately 1.7 million have been formally identified (including 4,200 mammal, 8,700 bird, 5,000 reptile, 21,000 fish, 400,000 plant, and 1.3 million invertebrate species). Over the history of life on this planet, species have continually come into existence and become extinct. It takes tens, even hundreds of thousands of years for a species to evolve. Up until the last 50,000 years, almost all extinctions were caused by nature. In the last 400 years, however, the rate of extinctions has risen dramatically due to human activities. Scientists estimate that by 1990 one species will become extinct every hour. Perhaps one-quarter or more of all existing species will be lost by the end of this century. Primary causes of extinction are human destruction or alteration of species habitat, and direct consumption of and commercial trade in live plants and animals and their products.

Preservation of species is essential to preserving genetic and biological diversity. At the very least this is of economic value to man. Genetic diversity in the wild is critical to survival through cross-breeding of many crops and animals on which we depend and will want to develop in the future. Biological diversity provides important sources of energy, industrial chemicals and raw materials, and medicines. Biological diversity may also be important to human psychology and underlies the philosophy that all life has value.

Various U.S. laws protect wildlife species and their habitats. The Endangered Species Act is the most important. It authorizes the federal government to identify threatened or endangered species, designate habitats critical to their survival, establish and conduct programs for their recovery, and control domestic trade and export and import of such species. It also prohibits federal actions that may jeopardize the existence of or modify the habitat of an endangered or threatened species. Under the act, a species is endangered if it is in danger of extinction and threatened if it is likely to become an endangered species within the foreseeable future.

There are also international protections, such as the Convention on International Trade in Endangered Species of Wild Fauna and Flora (CITES). CITES now has more than 95 member countries. They act by banning commercial trade in an agreed list of species most at risk of extinction and by regulating and monitoring trade in others that might become endangered.

Application of species protection laws is complicated by many factors. For example, a subspecies or individual population within a species in certain geographical areas may be threatened and be legally protected when other subspecies or populations of that same species in other locations are healthy and not protected.

and, shortly thereafter, in 1909, President Theodore Roosevelt declared almost 20 percent of the island as the Culebra National Wildlife Refuge. This was one of the first such refuge designations in a national system that now boasts more than 400 wildlife refuges. The island is an important nesting area for a wide variety of seabirds and several species of endangered sea turtles.

Like Palmas del Mar, Culebra has to be experienced firsthand to be fully appreciated. However, unlike Palmas, it didn't feel like a comfortable prison, but rather a modern-day, unspoiled Shangri-la. The island is inhabited by about 1800 Culebresans and a much smaller number of expatriate mainland Americans. Until 1976 the Navy used

A not so beautiful reminder of Culebra's beaches as a target range.

part of the island as a bombing target and as a consequence it wasn't high on the Caribbean list of tourist spots. Fortunately, the bombs didn't do any lasting damage to the scenery with the exception of a few bombed-out tanks strewn on the beaches, and since the end of the bombing, people have "discovered" this quiet, undeveloped, and extraordinarily beautiful paradise. Many of those who have come for a visit in recent years have managed to permanently delay their return to New York, Chicago, Maine, and other more hectic and less hospitable climes.

A chance meeting with Dulce, a young teacher of handicapped children on the island, led us to Jim, the local U.S. Fish and Wildlife Service representative, who then introduced us to Teresa, an Earthwatch project coordinator. It's a very small community and everyone knew everyone else.

For the past several years, Earthwatch has been monitoring sea turtle nesting on the remote Culebra beaches in cooperation with the Fish and Wildlife Service. Teresa leads groups of Earthwatch volunteers on daily and nightly patrols of remote beaches looking for turtle tracks and nesting turtles. The turtle tracks and nests are recorded for later visits during hatching time and then camouflaged to make it more difficult for poachers to find the eggs. Nesting turtles encountered during night patrols are measured and tagged as part of a large scale investigation of threatened and endangered sea turtles throughout the Caribbean. Teresa claimed that since the frequent beach patrols by Earthwatch volunteers, poaching of eggs and the illegal taking of the turtles for their meat and shells have declined by over 90 percent.

We joined Teresa on patrols of Resaca, Brava, and Zoni beaches. In addition to observing the Earthwatch project firsthand, it also gave us an opportunity to visit some spectacular and relatively inaccessible beach areas. In her short time on the island, Teresa had become an expert jeep driver over what barely pass as deeply rutted roads, and an equally accomplished mountain goat able to scamper over the steep foot paths that lead to the beaches. We didn't encounter any fresh tracks or nesting turtles, but I did run across a surprising amount of plastic debris on the beach.

Unlike my almost futile attempts to record observations of plastic debris in the open ocean on our 1,000-mile voyage to the Caribbean, here at the remote Culebra Wildlife Refuge, plastic debris was all over the place. There was an abundance of Styrofoam cups, pieces of discarded fishing nets, plastic straws, tampon applicators, plastic jugs

The Earthwatch turtle project coordinator in search of turtle tracks and nests. Photo by Scott Frankel.

of all sizes and shapes, shreds of plastic bags, packing straps, and miscellaneous pieces of plastic. In a 100-yard stretch along otherwise beautiful Flamenco Beach, I picked up about 10 percent of the plastic debris, which amounted to approximately one cubic foot of loosely packed material. For the whole two-mile beach, that would amount to about 320 cubic feet of plastic trash! I packed a sample of the evidence and mailed it back to the Center in Washington. The Culebra postal clerk asked if I wanted to insure the package.

It appeared from looking at the charts that much of the trash might have come from cruise ships, which travel back and forth from San Juan to the Virgin Islands and other Caribbean islands. The plastic debris data we collected on this voyage will be compared with other ocean debris data investigated by the Center to gain a better understanding of this problem. (See the appendix for more on the plastic debris problem.)

On our way back from Flamenco Beach, we had a humorous encounter with "Crazy" Jack, a dapper mainland expatriate with a well-groomed beard, who picked us up. We soon learned that Crazy Jack is the local raconteur and friendly car rental agent in Culebra. He had already given a lift to a young woman who sat in the front seat. We introduced ourselves as Michael and Scott from D.C. and San Francisco. While Crazy Jack was trying to tell us a bit about the zany, slow paced life on the island, she turned to us abruptly and asked, "Are you guys gay?"

We were so astonished at her remark that we never did find out whether the question was prompted by the fact that two men were traveling together, or that one of them was from San Francisco, or whether she just wanted company. I also didn't tell her that Scott was my son. We just ignored her for the rest of the ride and concentrated on Crazy Jack and his stories of Culebra.

There was another funny incident later that evening when Crazy Jack received a shipment of four motor scooters on the daily ferry from Puerto Rico. He enlisted three men at the bar to help him transport the scooters to his rental agency. Everyone at the bar was treated to a parade of brand-new, shiny, red scooters careening around the narrow pier and waterfront in the hands of inexperienced or inebriated drivers (or both) behind their leader, the dapper gentleman with the unusual handle of Crazy Jack.

All of our contacts on Culebra were with expatriate mainland Americans. Culebresans, I was told, are not particularly pleased with the influx of these mainlanders or with the environmental restrictions placed on their island as a result of the Wildlife Refuge management. Dulce, the teacher we had first met on the island, told us that the only way she had found to impress the Culebresans with environmental awareness about issues such as overfishing of conch and lobster, man-

The sportfishing armada from nearby Puerto Rico.

grove destruction for homesites, or turtle nesting protection was to educate the children, the next generation. We gladly gave Dulce several educational publications including a marine environment school curriculum and several Spanish-English coloring books on sea turtles.

We spent three nights on Culebra, taking in this unspoiled island, still free from possibly inevitable tourist development. The island boasts of a large, protected bay, which offers an uncrowded anchorage considered to be one of the best hurricane holes in the Caribbean. In fact, the anchorage is so good that the Navy kept a large fleet there until recently. Around the picturesque bay are several small guesthouse accommodations that would make a perfect hideaway to write that novel or to just laze around in the sun.

There have been strong rumors of a water pipeline from Puerto Rico to Culebra which would alleviate the chronic shortage of fresh water. Almost all the domestic water is captured in roof-top cisterns. A water pipeline would make it possible for a greatly expanded tourist economy. Real estate speculators are already busy. I was told that five-acre parcels were going for $50,000, and they were very hard to come by. With magnificent beaches, a very large and safe anchorage, proximity to an international airport in San Juan, and fresh water, tourism can't be far behind.

On our last night, we revisited Martas, the local watering hole at the foot of the town pier. Everyone who is anyone congregated here to ogle the latest crop of tourists just in on the ferry from Puerto Rico. On this night there was a special Japanese cookout prepared by the only Japanese person on the island. The meal wasn't very Japanese, but the decorations and the cook were authentic. We were also treated to a local amateur hour and one surprisingly good singer who mixed some rock 'n' roll, for the benefit of the Anglos, with his normal fare of Mexican ballads. It was a good ending to our visit to Shangri-la.

THE U.S. VIRGIN ISLANDS

We headed eastward in a 15-knot wind reaching toward the Virgins and American Paradise. The American Virgin Islands are the first group of islands in a string known as the Lesser Antilles, which curves southward, framing the Caribbean Sea all the way to South America.

It's a short 20-mile sail from Culebra to St. Thomas, the first of the U.S. Virgins in our path, but these two islands are culturally worlds apart. In contrast to the undeveloped, pristine, and wildlife-rich environment of Culebra, St. Thomas is a bustle of tourism, complete with all the popular fast-food chains and the well-known boutique jewelers and clothiers.

We anchored off Yacht Haven in Charlotte Amalie, a center for the "beautiful" people and their beautiful yachts. We saw quite a few luxury yachts, many of which were sporting satellite telephone antennas, no doubt to afford their owners instant access to Wall Street

The busy dinghy dock at Yacht Haven in St. Thomas.

brokers. The dockside lounge, directly on the pier, is one large empo-
rium of yacht groupies, either crew off their boats temporarily mixing
with their friends, or newcomers eagerly seeking a berth on a boat, or
charterers. One of the "in" products carried as a badge of success by
the yachties was a hand-held VHF radio to put them in instant touch
with the captain or crew docked a few feet away. *Sabra* and her crew
looked like "poor white trash" compared to these elegant yachts and
their gold-necklaced, VHF-toting crews.

While we waited for our 10 gallons of fuel at the dock, the
pleasure boat ahead of us took on 4,000 gallons of diesel! At the marina
office, where I was settling up my $17 fuel and water bill, the gentle-
man ahead of me was arranging six neat piles of hundred-dollar bills
to pay for his $6,000 charter bill! This was no place for Earthwatch
volunteers to be looking for turtle tracks.

We left St. Thomas and headed for St. John, where we were
invited to attend a United Nations dedication of the Biosphere Reserve
Center. St. John is the smallest of the U.S. Virgin Islands, about 20
square miles, with over 75 percent of the island designated as a national
park under the jurisdiction of the U.S. Park Service. Most of this
parkland was a gift from the Rockefellers at the time they developed
the elegant Caneel Bay resort. The park now buffers this resort from
surrounding development.

In 1976, UNESCO designated this park as a part of the international Biosphere Reserve system. The national park in St. John was
formally dedicated as a Biosphere Reserve in 1983 in recognition of
its international significance for research on the conservation of one of
the world's unique ecosystems. There are 41 other biosphere reserves
in the U.S. and about 250 worldwide. One of the intriguing aspects
of the St. John reserve is the opportunity to observe a fragile island
environment under extreme pressure from tourism development. In
managing the park and now the biosphere reserve, the Park Service has
the dual role of preserving a unique natural environment while at the
same time making the extraordinary beauty of the area available to the
public, and the public comes to this area in ever greater numbers.

The dedication formally opened the Biosphere Reserve Training
Center, where researchers are now able to study this ecosystem and
learn how best to manage its future development. The emphasis is on
protecting the indigenous wildlife and habitat and making as much of
it as possible available to the visiting public. One guest at the dedication remarked that this was quite a different attitude toward biosphere

A James Bond megayacht in St. Thomas.

reserves than in Russia, where only persons with a legitimate research project are permitted to enter a reserve. There the general public is only allowed to visit the museums and naturalist centers at the periphery, but not allowed into the actual reserve.

There were several speeches at the dedication addressing the opportunities presented by the reserve to redress past environmental abuses. A government representative from the nearby British Virgin Islands reminded everyone that Americans have used the area for many years without much regard for conservation. Lorna Smith was particularly concerned with anchor damage to coral beds and sea grasses, overfishing for deeper-water conch with scuba gear, and the clearing of mangrove stands to make way for bathing beaches. She reminded everyone that the days of Rockefeller resorts and large private parkland grants were a thing of the past. Now every available acre is up for development. She quipped that in America, an environmentalist is someone who already owns his second home. Here in the islands, she noted, the economy hasn't progressed as far so there are precious few environmentalists.

Carolyn Rogers, research biologist at St. John National Park, remarked that although the park has been in existence since 1956, very little research has been done on the environmental baseline of the park and the pressures of further development. She felt that more educational materials were needed to allow tourism to coexist safely with the park's natural environment. For example, she said, most boaters who indiscriminately drop their anchors don't realize that there may be life on the seabed getting crushed or gouged by the anchors. Interpretive brochures on anchoring to avoid damaging coral and sea grasses would be a very useful item for distribution to charter boat companies and at park service information booths.

In addition to brochures, Carolyn Rogers hoped to explore ways for private organizations to fund some of the research work needed to fulfill the promise of the Biosphere Reserve Center. Funds are needed to buy outright some of the unsecured holdings in the park to prevent further development within the reserve. Federal funds for these activities are very limited.

The dedication of the training center was a wonderful opportunity to meet scientists and administrators working on environmental issues in the Caribbean. It was also a good opportunity to have some hors d'oeuvres and drinks—a welcome change from our on-board cooking of several varieties of "gruel."

The next day, we motored to Caneel Bay to see how the "other half" lives and then on to Maho Bay for the night. The Danish tall ship *Danmark* was anchored off Caneel Bay preparing for the commemoration festivities of the transfer of the Virgin Islands from Danish to U.S. control in 1917. At that time the U.S. Virgins were bought for $25 million—not a bad deal for the American Paradise.

Maho Bay Camps on St. John is a unique resort in the islands since it features a living-with-nature theme. The rooms are platform tents and the entire campground is ringed with a network of wooden walkways built several feet over the natural terrain so as not to disturb the surroundings. The camp also features evening nature talks at the camp gazebo and nature field trips to augment the natural living experience.

Maho Bay and the adjoining Francis Bay are the sites of some extensive research on the decline of sea grasses. These beds are the

CORAL REEFS

Coral reefs exist in clear waters where there is high salinity and warm temperatures. A reef ecosystem may include up to 3,000 species of plants, invertebrates, and vertebrates including fish, worms, mollusks, algae, sponges, and urchins. The coral reef environment is primarily limited by space as many of the bottom-dwelling organisms, such as sponges, hard and soft corals, and algae, need a solid substrate on which to settle and grow. Holes and crevices in the substrate are important to the reef fish as shelter, spawning, and nursery grounds.

The hard or stony type of coral is closely related to anemones and "soft" corals, such as sea fans. The outer layer of a stony coral deposits a skeleton which is responsible for the reef building process. Reefs have the accumulated calcium carbonate remains of dead coral at the base with living coral found at the top and sides. Although the living coral are only at the surface of the reef mass, they are the most essential organism for the maintenance of the coral reef ecosystem.

The basic functional unit of any coral, hard or soft, is the polyp. Usually smaller than a pea, a polyp's soft tubelike body has a mouth fringed with many small tentacles that sting for defense and for capturing food.

Reef-building corals require sunlight and warm waters because they contain within their inner tissues microscopic algae which depend on photosynthesis to produce food for the host coral. Therefore, clear waters free of sediments induce healthy reef growth.

Successive generations of polyps remain attached to the original polyps and by constant addition of new buds, colonies are formed. For some species these colonies can reach several meters in diameter and live up to a 1,000 years.

Excess sedimentation, which reduces the clarity of the water, is a major threat to coral reefs. Sources for excess sedimentation are surface runoff from deforested and cleared areas, landfill, and dredging operations. Uncontrolled development such as road building, housing, and commercial development as well as industrial and agricultural pollution runoff are also serious threats to the well being of Florida and Caribbean coral reefs.

The Danish Tall Ship *Danmark* readies for the celebration commemorating the U.S. purchase of the Virgins.

habitat of one of the largest concentrations of the endangered green sea turtle in the Caribbean. The decline in sea grasses is attributed in large part to anchor damage from pleasure boats visiting these beautiful bays. Researchers have recommended restricting anchoring privileges in the area as a way of protecting the sea grasses and thus the endangered green sea turtle. Such a move would be met by fierce boater opposition. However, another possibility would be the installation of mooring buoys carefully placed and maintained by the Park Service. This would give boaters an opportunity to continue visiting the areas without further damaging the sea grasses. The only obstacle to the

mooring buoys would be their cost and the liability insurance needed
for their operation.

An even greater threat from anchors comes from the damage done
to coral beds by a new breed of "mini" cruise ships. The large cruise
ships, with a 1,000 or more tourists, tie up at piers or anchor in deep
waters. However, these new 200-passenger minicruisers anchor close to
shore to give their passengers a better view and more direct access to
the environment. Their anchors weigh more than 2,000 pounds and can
obliterate coral, sea grasses, and anything else in their way. By comparison, a typical pleasure craft anchor is in the 20- to 75-pound range.
Again, mooring buoys may be the answer for these ships. Cruise ship
operators might also be asked to pay for the buoys and their ongoing
maintenance.

ST. CROIX

We left St. John for an incredibly fast sail to St. Croix, 40 miles
away. We made the passage in less than seven hours, averaging more
than six knots. That's great for a 32-foot sailboat with a 2,000-year-old
rig design. I realize that doesn't sound like much when you're zipping
around the D.C. beltway or cruising the San Diego freeway at 65 mph,
but in a small sailboat it feels like rocket power and it doesn't cost a
cent in fuel.

St. Croix is the largest of the American Virgins and the home of
the nation's only underwater national park. To protect the magnificent
coral beds in this park, the Park Service provides mooring buoys for
the public and the tour boat operators. There are 10 such buoys and
they were fully occupied during our stay. It's clear that more will be
needed as the number of boaters increases.

Like the other U.S. Virgin Islands, St. Croix has experienced a
tourist development boom. The population growth rate on the islands
has been about 300 percent over the past 20 years. Several hotels were
under construction when we visited, and a local air traffic controller
who loaned us his mooring told me that the runway was being
extended to accommodate jumbo jets from Europe and the U.S. mainland. This will mean more tourists and cheaper fares to attract even
more tourists.

I don't think anyone knows what the tourist capacity is for the surrounding waters. Hopefully, the new biosphere reserve will provide an opportunity to conduct research not only on the development limitations of the Virgin Islands, but also on the controls needed to implement and enforce those limitations.

Our last day on St. Croix was spent snorkeling at Buck Island Underwater National Park. On the way back to the main island we had one of those rare times in sailing when everything is just perfect. *Sabra* ran the eight miles from Buck Island to Christiansted harbor with a beautiful outstretched wing-and-wing sailing configuration. We entered the busy harbor under sail and adroitly maneuvered around the many anchored and moored boats in search of the mooring buoy we had been using. We rounded up into the wind, dropped sails,

Children of St. Croix, U.S. Virgin Islands.

and picked up the buoy in one smooth, well-orchestrated motion.

I was intensely proud of the show we had put on for the tourists sitting in the lounges overlooking the harbor and walking along the waterfront as well as for the other boaters in the harbor enjoying a happy hour in their cockpits. *Sabra* and her new tanbark, junk-rigged sails looked great and somehow I felt that everyone was cheering the boat, skipper, and crew for a job well done.

The next day, we had another perfect, trade-wind sailing day on our return to St. Thomas. Before ending this leg of our trip, we made a quick side trip to the new Grand Hotel on St. John in Great Cruz Bay. This is the site of one of those mega-developments that creates so much pressure on the environment. Large mangrove stands, which form a critical habitat for the surrounding sea life, had had to give way for bathing beaches. Both the hotel development and the surrounding homes have caused considerable damage from uncontrolled sediment runoff which has injured coral, sea grasses, and other sea life. This is a prime example of high-impact tourism development (and without the compensation of donated parkland as was the case in Caneel Bay).

As I sailed deeper into the West Indies, it became more important to understand the local culture, especially as it relates to change, development, and pressures on the environment. In my readings I found this wonderful interpretation of the West Indian attitude toward change, actually penned 30 years ago by Herman Wouk, in his humorous novel, *Don't Stop The Carnival:*

> The West Indian is not exactly hostile to change, but he is not much inclined to believe in it. This comes from a piece of wisdom that his climate of eternal summer teaches him. It is that, under all the parade of human effort and noise, today is like yesterday, and tomorrow will be like today; that existence is a wheel of recurring patterns from which no one escapes; that all anybody does in this life is live for a while and then die for good, without finding out much; and that therefore the idea is to take things easy and enjoy the passing time under the sun. The white people charging hopefully around the islands these days in the noon glare, making deals, bulldozing airstrips, hammering up hotels, laying out marinas, opening new banks, night clubs, and gift shops, are to him merely a passing plague. They have come before and gone before.

Lorna Smith
and the B.V.I.

†††††

The British Virgin Islands

A fter a 10-day interlude, during which *Sabra* was moored in Red Hook, St. Thomas while I flew back to attend the Center's annual board meeting in Washington, D.C., we set sail for the British Virgin Islands. The brief trip home was a good opportunity to present an interim report on *Sabra*'s voyage. But I did feel guilty when people asked, "Are you still on that environmental whatchamacallit boondoggle?" You work hard to create a situation where you can combine work and pleasure and then you feel guilty about it. You can't win.

When I returned to *Sabra,* Kit joined us to help with the sailing and to add her environmental law experience to our observations. We continued the adventure across Drake Passage to the British Virgin Islands. The B.V.I. are a group of 38 islands with 12,000 inhabitants. Some of the islands are less than a mile from the neighboring U.S. Virgin Islands and the furthest is about 20 miles from St. John. Their proximity to the U.S. Virgins ties them inexorably to the same development pressures and impacts of tourist growth being experienced throughout the area.

THE BRITISH VIRGIN ISLANDS

We headed for Jost Van Dyke, a popular customs entry point for the B.V.I. As we approached the anchorage after a short motor-sail from St. Thomas, we saw our second endangered green sea turtle. The first turtle had been sighted in Red Hook, but we were too busy looking for our mooring to pay much attention to the turtle. Our second sighting was also short-lived because we were too busy looking

Mangrove roots under intensive study. Photo by Scott Frankel.

MANGROVES

The line between land and ocean is blurred considerably in mangrove forests. Here terrestrial plants have very successfully invaded the salt-water environment and created a productive environment that supports a broad array of animals. Like estuarine and wetland ecosystems, mangroves provide a rich source of food for commercially important fish and shellfish.

Mangroves are tropical species that grow best in tidal areas with little wave action. Mangroves can grow on sand, rock, and peat, but flourish in fine-grained soil composed of silt, clay, and organic matter. Bacteria, fungi, and other microorganisms cover fallen mangrove leaves, serving as a rich source of protein for shrimp, crabs, and some species of fish. Larger fish, turtles, dolphins, and birds, in turn, feed on these creatures.

Although the number of plant species in a mangrove community is small, the diversity of animal species is great. In part, this is because mangrove communities are borders between marine and terrestrial ecosystems. Such transitional ecosystems have a greater diversity than the communities lying on either side of them. They may be inhabited by species from each of the flanking communities as well as species not found in either.

Mangroves are valuable as nursery grounds for commercially valuable fish and shellfish, for protection of coastal areas from stormwaters, for the conservation of threatened and endangered species, and for tourism.

Concrete blocks and sand ready to replace mangroves.

for our cameras. We decided to not worry about photographs the next time we saw one. They're quite beautiful to watch as they gracefully swim just beneath the water with their heads bobbing for air every few minutes. A green sea turtle can be more than a yard long and weigh over 200 pounds. The harbor has several patches of sea grasses which provide the green sea turtle's primary diet.

The mangrove trees along the shore of this harbor are slowly but steadily being replaced by small development projects. We saw several piles of concrete building blocks and construction sand about to replace more of these trees. The mangroves, as well as the sea grasses, constitute a critical habitat for a wide variety of sea life. In the Caribbean, these plants along the shoreline act in the same way as wetland marshes do in the northern latitudes.

Customs procedures in the B.V.I. are very straightforward. Some-one once said that the only countries worth visiting, if you want a minimum of bureaucratic hassle, are those that were previously, or are still, occupied by the British. Somehow they were able to install a reasonable and rational civil service which survived their rule and domination. For *Sabra,* the customs process was simply the filling out of three forms and a payment of $8.83. No passports or ship's papers were required, and the forms covered both our entry to the B.V.I. and our exit several days hence.

Homemade boogie-board on Jost Van Dyke, British Virgin Islands.

From Jost Van Dyke we sailed to Sopers Hole on the main island of Tortola. This quiet little anchorage, which I remembered from an earlier visit in 1982, had undergone considerable shoreline development. There was a fancier restaurant replacing the funky grass hut watering hole, a yacht club with adjoining pier, and a complete haul-out facility for yacht maintenance. Unnoticed, we tied up at the yacht club pier and saved ourselves the cost of an overnight mooring or the hassle of anchoring in the deep water of the harbor. Manually hauling up heavy anchor chain can get very old.

The next morning, we motored the five miles to Road Town, the capital of Tortola. Here we had an appointment with the ministry of natural resources to hear about environmental problems in the B.V.I. We elected to tie up at a respectable marina so that we could shed our sail-bum appearance and get thoroughly cleaned up for a meeting at the ministry.

The Village Cay Marina was very elegant at 70 cents per foot, per night. This included the right to a five-minute hot shower—for an additional two dollars. Tokens had to be secured from the marina office to operate the water meter on the shower. On my personal scale of showers this one ranked as an abbreviated Number 5. It was hot and clean, but five minutes is a bit short, especially for one who likes to think and shave in the shower.

The marina was well situated, being only 15 minutes from the ministry and 25 minutes from an excellent pizza establishment. The lazy walk to the pizza parlor included a stop at a previously undiscovered supermarket where we greedily cornered the island's available supply of granola cereal.

THE MINISTRY OF NATURAL RESOURCES

All cleaned, shaved, and dressed in long white slacks, dressy short-sleeved shirt, and white tennies, I headed for the Ministry. (I point out my attire only because it's such a problem deciding what to wear to a business meeting in this heat and casual atmosphere.)

Lorna Smith, the permanent secretary of the Ministry of Natural Resources, and Dr. Nicholas Clarke, the director of the National Parks Trust, provided an overview of the marine environment of the B.V.I. and the pressures facing this environment from a growing tourism-dependent economy. Two specific problems discussed were overfishing to meet the insatiable food demands of tourists and reef damage caused by anchoring and physical contact between boats and fragile coral reefs.

I learned that there are sufficient laws and regulations to control these problems, but there are insufficient funds to monitor, enforce, or publicize the problems and the need for cooperative actions. Characteristically, the majority of government funding is directed at tourism development but not the environmental impact of this development. A good measure of this inequity is the five-to-one ratio of government funding for the Department of Tourism vs. the Natural Resource Ministry. Lorna Smith observed that local politicians view support of development and protection against the environmental impacts of that development as separate and competing interests, rather than simply two sides of the same issue.

One of the measures that has been taken by the B.V.I. government to draw attention to environmental protection is the designation of national parks through the National Parks Trust. This is a statutory body established by the government for the management of natural terrestrial, marine, and historic resources in protected areas. The trust identifies valuable areas and administers management projects in those areas. In effect the trust operates in a manner similar to the U.S. Park Service. The trust was started in the early 1960s, at the beginning of the yachting boom, following a land gift from the Rockefellers, who developed Little Dix Bay, the first major resort hotel in the B.V.I. The Rockefellers had a similar environmental conservation impact on St. John in the American Virgins following the development of the Caneel Bay Resort. This strongly suggests that it takes a single deep-pocketed philanthropic organization with a conservation vision to get the ball rolling.

The National Parks Trust is now funded by the government and private donations. The Jackson Hole Preserve, Inc., and the World Wildlife Fund are two of the trust's funding sources. In 1987, a new group called Friends of the National Parks Trust was established to raise additional funds and to make the public aware of the trust's activities. The newsletter of this organization includes description of trust projects as well as proposed projects for which funds are needed. In the newsletter, U.S. citizens are encouraged to make tax-deductible donations to the trust through the U.S.-based World Wildlife Fund.

One marine park has been designated and seven others have been proposed by the B.V.I. government. The designated park commemo-rates the sinking of the Royal Mail Steamer *Rhone,* which was driven onto the rocks of Salt Island by a hurricane in 1867 with a loss of 125 people. The wreck is now encrusted with marine life and forms a popular dive site. To preserve the wreck and the coral reef formed by the wreck, the government has placed over a dozen mooring buoys in the area for both tourist vessels and commercial dive operators. This step was taken to prevent the increasing damage caused by improper anchoring. Dr. Clarke was quick to point out that one of the concerns with the government buoys was the government's legal liability in

A mooring buoy provided by the British Virgin Island government to protect a valuable coral reef.

Users of government-owned buoys are cautioned.

maintaining these buoys. A similar sentiment was expressed by Carolyn Rogers of the U.S. Park Service in neighboring St. John, when asked why the Park Service didn't place moorings in the endangered sea grass areas of Maho Bay. It appears that some form of "hold harmless" ruling will have to be enacted if governments are to install any more of these simple and effective moorings.

Later, during our cruising of the B.V.I., we stopped on our way to Virgin Gorda at the Wreck of the Rhone Marine Park to photograph the buoys. The first buoy we approached was missing its pendant. Someone must have driven over it with a propeller. All the buoys were marked with an "at your own risk" message.

MOORINGS TO PROTECT CORAL AND SEA GRASSES

Coral reefs are an underwater fantasy garden of rainbow-hued fish, swaying sea fans and coral splashed with color. For thousands of years the reefs have withstood natural stresses, only to face the most devastating threat of all—boat anchors and their chains. Today, in many nearshore waters, hundreds of years of coral growth are destroyed in a few hours. Protecting the beauty of the reefs of Florida and the Virgin Islands will require mooring buoys installed at strategic points, for use by charter and dive boats as well as tourists and locals. These anchoring buoys would allow those of us who enjoy the reefs to continue visiting them without damaging the coral and sea grasses.

Key Largo and Looe Key National Marine Sanctuaries have already established regulations to fine boat owners whose anchors damage any part of the sanctuary. Buck Island Reef National Monument and Coral Reef State Park are two of the state parks and local areas which have passed regulations to protect their coral. There are still, however, many reefs unprotected by such laws.

Although coral reefs are extensive, they grow very slowly. What you actually see when diving is the thin layer of live coral on top of the nonliving skeleton. Recent research indicates that it takes 250 to 500 years for the coral heads of a reef to grow seven feet high. Thus, an irresponsible skipper can easily wipe out 500 years worth of growth, by knocking down the castle-like coral heads in one shattering encounter. If a boat drifts or swings on its anchor, the chain will grind on the ocean floor, destroying any coral or sea grass in its path.

A comparison of 1960 maps of sea grass beds with grass beds today near anchoring sites shows that grasses have been greatly reduced. The disruption of this ecosystem is devastating to the sea turtles, fish, and other organisms dependent on the grasses for survival.

The state parks, the national marine sanctuaries, and the national monuments of Florida and the Virgin Islands are beginning to act on the anchoring problem. Mooring buoys and anchoring regulations are coming into widespread use to protect the sea grasses and coral, to regulate the carrying capacity of the area, and to educate the public about their impact on the beautiful, yet fragile reefs. Still, more literature and signs are needed to further educate the public on the need for mooring buoys.

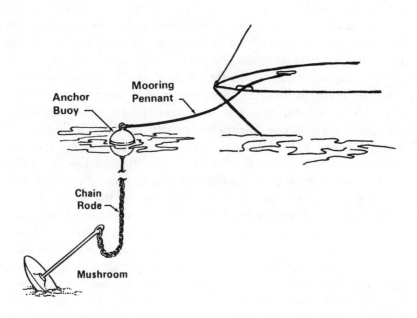

Lorna Smith pointed out that although the American and British Virgins are close together and share most of the same tourists, there is limited collaboration on the definition of environmental problems caused by tourism or on developing solutions to these problems. There have been some cooperative research and environmental surveys but no concrete results. The newly designated United Nations Biosphere Reserve in St. John, whose sphere of influence covers the B.V.I., is a possible framework for future cooperative projects but no such agendas had yet been developed.

According to Lorna Smith, the primary, local nongovernment organization (NGO) interested in the marine environment has been the B.V.I. Dive Operators Association, which has been very helpful in surveying valuable underwater resources and educating its members on the protection of these resources. The association has also helped to survey coral reef areas eventually to be designated off-limits to the minicruise ships, which tend to anchor too close to the reefs. The newly formed Friends of the National Trust may prove to be another valuable local NGO to help designate and protect important marine resources. Both Lorna and Nick hoped that NGOs would help to fund such activities as the publication of leaflets, posters, brochures, and other instructional and consciousness-raising materials to assist in protecting the marine environment. The sea turtle coloring book and the sea turtle poster prepared by the Center were in wide use in the B.V.I. and were cited as examples of outside NGO assistance to governmental efforts.

In connection with sea turtles, Dr. Clarke pointed out that there was a documented leatherback nesting area on the north coast of Tortola where fishermen regularly took these endangered turtles for their oil, known as trunk oil. This oil is reputed to have medicinal qualities similar to castor oil. One interesting aside I learned was that the local fishermen, after killing a female leatherback with eggs, would bury the eggs in the hope of perpetuating their source of supply. Unfortunately, there is no evidence to suggest that this human intervention is effective. The B.V.I. government recognizes the need to restrict the taking of sea turtles and has begun to impose taking seasons. However, the long-standing practice of catching turtles year-round created political opposition to restrictions.

At the time of my visit, the B.V.I. government had no plans to send a representative to the upcoming CITES (Convention on International Trade in Endangered Species of Wild Fauna and Flora) meeting because of the expense. They also felt that the rules of this convention, aimed at curbing trade in such items as tortoiseshell and certain corals, were too complicated to follow, especially by their customs officials. The B.V.I. would appear to be another good target area for interpretive brochures, pamphlets, and training materials that could be prepared by an outside organization for use by many island governments.

PETER ISLAND AND VIRGIN GORDA

The next day, following another good pizza dinner, we headed for Peter Island to savor one of those perfect Caribbean beaches. Here, as in Tortola and later in Virgin Gorda, we encountered a large number of Puerto Rican tourists in powerboats. Americans are clearly the predominant tourist group in the B.V.I. The first step in marine conservation for the B.V.I. is to reach these tourists. Yacht charters from the American Virgins, American dive operators, American sportfishermen, American cruise ship operators and passengers, and the American publishers of cruising guides need to embrace and pass on the message of marine conservation. A simple explanation of anchoring etiquette in valuable coral reef and sea grass areas published in yacht cruising guides would be a start.

After a very peaceful, star-filled night at Deadman's Cove on Peter Island, we sailed smartly off our anchor for Salt Island and another brief visit at the Wreck of the Rhone Marine Park. From there we had a beautiful reach to Virgin Gorda, where we tied up at the marina for the night. We were looking forward to another shower and some laundromat action. It seemed that certain pleasures and necessities of life had a great influence on schedules and choice of stops.

Sailing in the B.V.I., and the American Virgins for that matter, is a wonderful experience. The waters are well protected, there are plenty of safe anchorages, and land-based amenities are never very far away. You don't have to venture deeper into the Caribbean, especially on short vacations, to get the full measure of trade-wind sailing and the charm of island hopping. There may be more beautiful and desolate spots, more of a foreign ambience, and more exhilarating sailing, but the hassles increase commensurately as one proceeds down-island.

The Easter weekend on Virgin Gorda held a special treat for us

The crew sticks close to the chart.

in the form of a local West Indian calypso, soca, and reggae concert. The electric music was loud and throbbing, and the crowd of locals and tourists was very entertaining.

Mingling in the crowd of dancers and listeners were two con artists with a variation of the ancient shell game. Each had a small pedestal table and three plastic disks. One of the disks had chalk markings on its underside. The con artists would shuffle the disks with great flourishes and exaggerated arm motions finally flinging the disks on the small table area. The audience would then plunk down $20, $50, and $100 bills on a single guess of the odd disk. These folks really seemed to enjoy blowing a few hundred dollars on this game. We noted that many of the well-healed bettors were Puerto Rican tourists having motored over from Puerto Rico in very large sportfishing boats.

The next morning, we headed for Gorda Sound and the Bitter End, Biras Creek, and Tradewinds resorts. All three of these resorts are tucked away in the southwestern corner of the Sound next to beautiful reefs off the private islands of Necher and Eustatia. We spent the day touring the resorts, snorkeling, and observing the environmental effects of these developments. There were some particularly good photographic opportunities to capture a solitary mangrove tree surrounded

A solitary mangrove.

by a well landscaped and well groomed beach. It was another reminder of the mangrove destruction that takes place to make room for resort beaches.

When I asked a sports activity staff member for directions to the best snorkeling site, he pointed to the area and told me to simply tie my dinghy off on the coral heads. I found it hard to believe this advice, given the damage that can be done to the fragile coral which takes hundreds of years to grow. I repeated the question to the director of the office, and he suggested I anchor in the sand and swim to the coral. I guess environmental protection wasn't in the job description yet among the hotel staff.

They're Rioting
in Marigot

†††††

Virgin Islands to St. Kitts

A fter several delightful days in Gorda Sound, *Sabra* slipped her moorings for yet another of those windward slogs. This time across the infamous Anegada Passage. Our destination was St. Martin/Sint Maarten, the island split between the French and Dutch nations.

We were hoping that this crossing would be the last lengthy windward passage for a long while. Sometimes the boat and crew really took a beating going against the persistent easterly trade winds, with various bolts, nuts, or hose clamps coming loose as we bashed against the waves. And unlike the brisk off-wind passages, on the windward legs it seemed as though the last landmark wouldn't let go and the next one refused to arrive.

The range of islands between the Virgins and Dominica are referred to as the Leeward Islands, and those below Dominica all the way to South America are referred to as the Windward Islands.

Cruising Guide to the Caribbean and the Bahamas, by J. Hart and W. Stone, extols the Leeward Island region for its perfect layout with only a day's sail between islands. However, the guide goes on to caution that the only imperfection in this sailing paradise was the Anegada Passage:

When the Caribbean islands burst through into the sunlight, the gods in charge of the area must have had a pretty keen sailor on the board of directors. Admittedly, someone blundered a little in the vicinity of the Anegada Passage, but on the whole, the islands stretch away to the south an amazingly regular 20 miles apart and at a handy right angle to the bustling trade winds. The lee coasts have an abundance of perfect harbors, usually strategically placed at either end of the islands, and most of the loose bits of rock, which in the beginning must have splattered around, fell into deep enough water not to be a nuisance.

The passage is about 100 miles wide and on an eastward bound voyage, must be crossed directly into the wind. I debated over heading southward from Virgin Gorda and then tacking northward to St. Martin or heading northward and then southward. In either case it was going to be a long, slow overnight passage.

The north-then-south passage won out because there was a chance of making an overnight stop at Sombrero Island, midway across the Anegada Passage. This small rock of an island, 40 feet tall and a few hundred yards long, would provide a lee shore for a brief overnight anchorage. Besides the protection from the wind, the island also has a powerful light beacon, making it easy to find in the dark.

With all the plans having been made and the SatNav, or "Mr. Sulu," as it was now being called, in good working order, we left our quiet mooring at the Bitter End Yacht Club and prepared once more to do battle with the easterly trades.

It's interesting how inanimate machinery aboard a boat gets named and talked to or talked about as though it were a live member of the crew. In addition to Mr. Sulu, of "Star Trek" fame, we were accompanied by Pierre, the French wind vane, and Sir Sedwick, the British autopilot. In case the electronic instruments failed, I also had stowed away Chris Columbus, the Dutch chip log, and Mark Twain, the lead line. All these crew members were invaluable in their uncomplaining and unfailing service.

Beating against the trades and the ocean swells was getting to be an all too common experience. After each windward passage, I reflected on the punishment boat and crew were taking, and I was reminded of Chay Blyth, a crazy Englishman who chose to set a sailing record by going around the world singlehanded against the prevailing winds. You would have to be crazy to endure this type of bashing for eight months. (Incidentally, Blyth was also crazy enough to row across the Atlantic on another of his adventures.)

I was only doing it for a few days at a time with the constant promise that soon we would "turn the corner" and the remainder of the trip would be a downhill sleigh ride. We headed out into the Anegada Passage full of cheer, looking for that "corner."

About 1 A.M. we finally saw the beacon at Sombrero Island. As we approached it, the light became very bright and it looked dangerously close. Mr. Sulu indicated that the island was still 10 miles away, yet it looked very much closer. Around 2 A.M. I realized that I would never be able to see the rock until I was literally upon it so we decided to forego the temporary anchorage, give the rock a wide berth, and make straight for St. Martin.

ST. MARTIN/SINT MAARTEN

Finally, around dusk that day we approached Philipsburg, the main port and capital of Sint Maarten, the Dutch half of the island. Philipsburg won the toss over Marigot on the French side because it promised a quaint Dutch village atmosphere. As it turned out, Marigot was a much quainter village with a real foreign ambience. Philipsburg, on the other hand, was a very commercial town catering to the shop-hungry cruise ship tourists.

Since we arrived so late in the day, the customs office was closed. We checked in with the police who told us to come back in the morning for the clearance process. We were advised by the cruising guides that customs procedure gets to be a much more serious and a much bigger deal after leaving the Virgins, but apparently the Dutch were quite casual about it. We didn't want to go back to the boat empty-handed so we bought a couple of Haagen Daz ice cream cones—it sounded like a product from that part of the world even though we knew it to come from Brooklyn via Pillsbury—Ben and Jerry's had not made it to Philipsburg yet.

The anchorage was very rolly due to the swells and it wasn't until our second night in Philipsburg, when we set a second anchor to point the boat into the swells, that we had a comfortable night's sleep. The town itself wasn't much more pleasant than the rolling anchorage. We

Would you believe, "cabinet-maker-alley"?

did find a wonderful pizza parlor right on the waterfront and after finishing our first pizza we ordered a second one because we didn't want to leave the pleasant surroundings. The further we were from home, the more of a pizza craving we were experiencing.

The next day we checked in with customs and were treated to an unexpected chuckle. The man ahead of me told the official that he had a little problem. It seems that he arrived on St. Martin a few months ago on a sailboat. He had cleared customs with a young lady friend who was listed as a crew member. Since their arrival they had split up and to his knowledge she was carrying on with another gentleman on the island. He now wished to be relieved of any responsibility for his former friend and crew member. He sheepishly acknowledged that she was making quite a scene on the island and he did not want to get in trouble with the authorities over her actions. The customs official was sympathetic and assured the worried skipper that he would not be held accountable for her indiscretions. In comparison to this little drama, our entry was quite blasé, and at no cost we were officially cleared for both the Dutch and French portions of St. Martin.

On each of the islands, we picked up the local tourist brochures in search of any special messages regarding the protection of that island's fragile environment. The brochures also complemented the cruising guides with up-to-date information on things to do and the location of the nearest ice cream parlor and pizza establishment. One unforgettable line in the St. Martin guidebook must have lost something in the translation . . .

To make you feel even more at home in St. Maarten's beautiful casinos we give you a short explanation of the three major games being played in St. Maarten, apart from the slot pleasure which is self-explaining. . .

MARIGOT, ST. MARTIN

After taking our fill of the Dutch T-shirt shops, duty-free jewelry, and electronic gadget shops we decided to take a jitney bus across the island to the French Saint Martin. We were looking for the continental Caribbean: European charm, wharfside bistros, friendly people, and quiet streets.

The jitney was forced to let us off a few blocks from town due to heavy traffic. We found ourselves in a traffic gridlock reminiscent of New York or Los Angeles. We started walking and soon noticed crowds of people lined up on the sidewalks and along the streets. We also saw quite a few intersections blocked off with junked car chassis, tires, and other debris.

We asked several onlookers what was going on. Was there a parade or a carnival about to happen? They said they didn't know. It was curious that people would be milling around not knowing what was happening. However, the question was soon answered as a platoon of French riot police came trotting along with their plastic shields, batons, gas masks, and tear gas launchers. We were in the middle of a riot!

The official St. Martin tour guide says that the Marigot French gendarmes are a "police force of seven," that "spends almost all of the time greeting visitors." Well, today they had a few other duties, including building protective barricades and launching a tear gas grenade into the crowd. By U.S. standards it was a very small riot. Only one tear gas canister was fired and most of the crowd wasn't doing much other than belligerently milling about. It was strange to see obscenities hurled in French at what looked like the Foreign Legion in short pants. "Mother———" sounds so civilized in a French accent. It was a verbal standoff.

A few European spectators, roused from the boutiques and waterside bistros, joined the crowds as the gendarmes tried to negotiate with the locals and clear the streets. After awhile most of the spectators got bored and drifted back to the boutiques and bistros. We joined them for a Perrier and some serious people-watching. The French, and especially the women, have a way of dressing that invites ogling. Fortunately for us, miniskirts and very minishorts are de rigueur in this climate and the women were making the least of it. We had a ringside seat in a pleasant bistro overlooking a quaint harbor full of sailboats.

We headed back toward the riot area to take a picture and to find our way back to the bus. The crowds had thinned some but the riot squad was still on duty and the gendarmes in their dress shorts were seriously negotiating with the rioters. It wasn't till the next day's paper appeared that we finally learned what the riot was all about. It said that the riot was in response to the gendarmes' demolition of recently built, low-income housing. The housing, according to the paper, was built without permits and the authorities are cracking down on unauthorized construction.

There were no buses around so we decided to hitch a ride. The thumb is a handy device for boat people stranded on land. Luckily, we scored a direct hit with a delightful couple from Massachusetts. They were touring the island in a rented car, well armed with maps and advice from a local tour consultant, and, even more important, with a keen curiosity and a sense of adventure.

While Scott, Kit, and I sat in the back seat, Judy drove and Brendan was alternating between sunglasses and reading glasses as he tried to read road maps and navigate the narrow, unmarked roads. Behind the wheel, Judy was not to be intimidated by the locals' unpredictable driving. Their willingness to give us a ride back to

A riot in paradise—Marigot, St. Martin.

Philipsburg was welcome enough to us. The marvelous surprise was their invitation, which we gladly accepted, to continue on around the entire island. By the time this ride was to end we would have completed a circumnavigation of Saint Martin/Sint Maarten.

We spent the afternoon seeing peaceful beaches, hotels, quiet lagoons, lots of goats, small seaside towns, and miles of old stone walls reminiscent of the Middleburg, Virginia countryside. At one point during the ride, on the Dutch side, we spotted a market with a billboard advertising fish and turtle meat. We photographed the sign for further evidence of turtle taking in the Caribbean. It was very pleasant that the only formalities to be observed in crossing the island's Dutch-French border were the flags and roadside sign welcoming you to another country.

But without doubt the most rewarding aspect of this unplanned tour was the new friends we had made in the process, however briefly.

On our last day in Philipsburg we went shopping for a few necessities, particularly a new set of oars. We had lost our dinghy oars in the night when the heavy swells apparently combined with a stray gust and upturned the dinghy. In the morning we found the inverted dinghy *sans* oars. That was an expensive lesson. From then on we stowed the oars on board instead of in the dinghy. I also managed to lose my deck shoes. In an effort to keep them dry, I had taken them

Sea turtle meat for sale in Philipsburg, Sint Maarten.

St. Barts, a very picturesque French island.

off on the pier before boarding the perpetually wet dinghy. And like a fool I left them there after scrambling down the concrete pier. Unlike stowing the oars on the boat, I had no convenient way to avoid a recurrence of this loss unless I tie a string between each shoe and through my shorts the way mothers tie mittens to forgetful children.

ST. BARTS

From St. Martin we headed southeastward toward St. Barts. It was less than 20 miles to this French island, but again the trades extended

St. Barts architecture.

A view from a hotel lounge on St. Barts.

the trip to an all-day slog. We finally arrived at Gustavia, the main port of entry for St. Barts. This was the first postcard harbor we had encountered on this trip. The small harbor was nestled in the middle of town with the surrounding hills completely blocking the winds and swells.

The atmosphere on St. Barts was strictly French. We sat at a corner cafe watching people and drinking in the ambience of this European styled port. We had tried to check in with customs but the gendarmes were singularly uninterested in our entry. As it turned out, we entered and left St. Barts two days later without ever making contact with customs or immigration officials.

The next day, bright and early, I dinghied ashore and picked up hot-out-of-the-oven croissants for breakfast. During a walk later in the day we met a "local," a former boat delivery captain from Texas, who now makes his living running a combination print shop and ice company. He gave us some good advice regarding our next stops, St. Kitts and Nevis. As far as the harbors were concerned, he said, Charlestown, Nevis was the lesser of two evils.

A seashore car dump in St. Barts.

ST. KITTS AND NEVIS

We left St. Barts intending to make Charlestown, Nevis in one day. However, those contrary trades again forced a change in plans and we stopped at isolated Major Bay on the undeveloped side of St. Kitts. This turned out to be a pleasant surprise. We arrived at dusk to find the bay entirely deserted. It was actually kind of eerie to be the only boat in this remote anchorage on a remote part of the island. Our imagination allowed us to pretend that we had just made a difficult landfall in the remotest region of Antarctica—during a warm spell.

It was a very still night under a bright, starry sky, totally unmarred by any terrestrial lights. In the morning, after a wonderfully quiet night, we took the dinghy ashore and explored the lonely beach before continuing on to Nevis. The only thing marring this idyllic spot was the large quantity of plastic trash on the beach. It is impossible to escape the plastic packing straps, jugs, six-pack ring holders, discarded fishing nets, Styrofoam cups, and plastic bags. I am now convinced that there are huge quantities of this plastic trash in the ocean based on the quantities I found on small, remote beaches. Even though one can't see much of this litter while out in the ocean itself, and the water looks so crystal clear and clean around the islands, the beaches manage to receive large quantities of this insidious trash.

After our tour of the beach we set out under motor for the four-mile crossing to Charlestown, Nevis. As promised, the harbor wasn't much. It was a roadstead without protection from wind or swells. Fortunately, the seas were relatively calm and at least the wind and swells were in the same direction. It took several office stops in separate buildings to clear customs. First, there was the customs office to clear the boat, then immigration to clear the crew, and lastly the police for good measure. After all three offices were happy with our paperwork and our $20, we spent a few minutes touring the small town and settled down for lunch. We noticed that tortoiseshell products were for sale at a local crafts center and a complete turtle shell was for sale at the restaurant. Nevis was not a regular stop for cruise ships and it didn't rate very high as a sailing stopover, so there was very little in the way of commercial development. The town was quite unattractive, except for the well cared for home of Alexander Hamilton, so we made plans to tour Basseterre, St. Kitts, the next day before moving on to Antigua.

Instead of sailing to St. Kitts and suffering through another bad anchorage, we elected to take a 40-minute ferry ride to the neighboring port. Nevis and St. Kitts are part of the same country so there were no additional clearance procedures to go through.

Our first stop in Basseterre was the local bakery, where we had breakfast before our meeting at the attorney general's office. Mr. D.L. Mendis, an Indian civil servant on loan from the United Nations, spent several hours with us explaining the new environmental laws on St. Kitts and Nevis. Mr. Mendis was an attorney and legislative draftsman.

A serious grounding on Nevis.

He said that the legislature had passed the Environmental Protection and Conservation Act of 1987, which among other things established a commission to define and set up protected areas for unique and valued historic as well as environmental resources. A new regulation had also been written under the fisheries law that established a five-year moratorium on the taking of sea turtles, sea turtle eggs, or interfering in any way with sea turtle nesting.

Mr. Mendis said there was growing pressure within the government to deal with environmental and natural resource questions. A major reason for this pressure was a new road under development linking Basseterre and the hitherto remote and largely inaccessible area of southern St. Kitts. The road was being funded by U.S. AID and, as a result of U.S. laws, environmental impact assessments had to be made before the funds were released to construct the road. So in effect, the U.S.'s institutionalized awareness of the environmental consequences of road development was encouraging the St. Kitts government to deal with its own natural resources.

When asked if St. Kitts planned to accede to the CITES Convention to prevent international trade in endangered species, he said that under St. Kitts law, becoming a party to the convention wouldn't automatically result in laws to protect these species. The CITES conventions would have to be worked into Kittitian laws and that would be very difficult. He felt the convention was too complicated to be incorporated. This was the second reference I'd heard to CITES being too complicated for local administration. I'd heard the same thing in the B.V.I. There seemed to be a need and an opportunity to provide training or to redefine limited aspects of CITES that could be readily implemented by these small island nations.

Another of Mr. Mendis's concerns was marine pollution, particularly oil spills from tankers that regularly pass this region from Trinidad and Tobago. He indicated that more research was underway in this area. Similarly, more work needed to be done regarding the dumping of garbage by cruise ships, although he saw no problem in gaining the cruise ship industry's cooperation to solve this problem.

Mr. Mendis said he would be most appreciative if outside environmental groups could provide training materials and research materials for use by the government, particularly in implementing CITES regulations.

Mr. Mendis was very generous with his time. I got the feeling that our unannounced meeting was the most important thing on his calen-

CITES—CONVENTION ON INTERNATIONAL TRADE IN ENDANGERED SPECIES OF WILD FAUNA AND FLORA

Trade in live wildlife and wildlife products around the world is a varied, complex multibillion-dollar industry. In 1973, in response to fears that unregulated international trade was threatening the survival of many wildlife species, CITES was concluded to bring this trade under control. Appendix I of this treaty lists species threatened with extinction which are or may be affected by commercial trade, such as the great whales and all species of sea turtles. Species on this list are prohibited from international commercial trade except under exceptional circumstances. Appendix II lists less threatened species, such as black coral, which are not threatened but might become so if trade is not controlled. Trade in these species is permitted but must be authorized by the government of the country of origin. Species on this list require the issuance of an export permit from the country of origin.

CITES, like other international treaties, establishes a framework for participation by member governments. CITES is headquartered in Switzerland, and members meet every two years to decide on changes in species listings and to discuss issues relative to the treaty's implementation. Each member country has one vote. There are 95 participating countries in this convention. Of the 29 countries in the wider Caribbean, only four, the Bahamas, Dominican Republic, Trinidad and Tobago, and St. Lucia, are members.

Increasing industrial, commercial, and agricultural development of Caribbean islands and growing human populations with pressing subsistence needs are taking their toll on the wildlife of many Caribbean islands. These pressures, coupled with international trade, have brought many Caribbean species, birds and reptiles especially, close to extinction, and others are on their way. Because island ecosystems are so fragile, the loss of a single species can have disastrous effects on the entire ecosystem, imperiling many other species as well.

For Caribbean countries whose ocean borders are difficult to police and their law enforcement resources limited, CITES forms the basis for cooperation in protecting endangered wildlife, while it also provides a mechanism for assessing the volume of trade and the effect it may have on wildlife populations. For example, in 1987 the total tonnage of hawksbill shells exported to Japan from the Caribbean represented the taking of over 10,000 endangered sea turtles and moved this species that much closer to extinction!

Conch are becoming threatened in some areas because of
overfishing to feed the tourists and the introduction of scuba gear
to fish in deeper waters.

dar that day, or maybe that week. Sitting in his office, surrounded by
dusty law books and listening to his Indian accent, I also got the feeling
that I was back in the British colonial period in India. I must have seen
too many episodes of "Jewel in the Crown."

Before our next meeting with Ricky Skerrit of the Chamber of
Industry and Commerce, we walked the town and noted several shops
selling tortoiseshell jewelry. I wondered how the new rules prohibiting
turtle taking would affect this business. We also noticed a remarkable
difference between the neatly landscaped hotel district and the dust,

dirt, and open sewers of the rest of the town. The differences in quality of life were glaring.

Our meeting with Mr. Skerrit reaffirmed what we had learned earlier about the role of U.S. AID funds and the new environmental awareness of the St. Kitts government. He noted that the government had made an announcement over the radio that day asking people not to pick up endangered black coral. This was in direct response to a petition circulated by a local fisherman and conservationist. This was the first such public statement on the marine environment by the government.

Mr. Skerrit said that tourism would continue to grow on the

Brain coral in Majors Bay, St. Kitts.

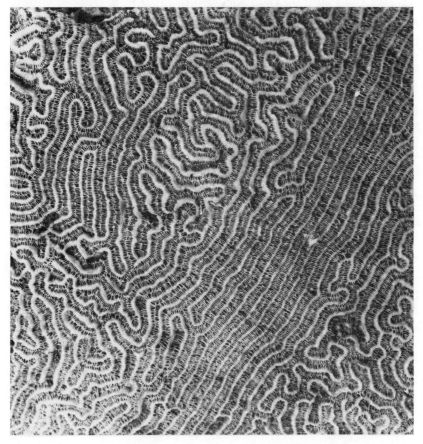

islands at a 15- to 20-percent rate over the next few years with most of the investments coming from North America. One of the side issues connected with this growth was the growing need for sand for construction. Mining the sand for hotel construction had the double effect of deteriorating the natural beauty which attracted the developers in the first place and destroying the nesting areas for sea turtles. He pointed out that it was difficult to enforce sand mining regulations in the face of the costly alternative to trucking sand over long distances.

The general public is largely unaware of environmental problems, according to Mr. Skerrit. However, local businessmen and politicians are beginning to appreciate the need to protect their natural environment. Pressures to introduce more environmental legislation and to enforce existing legislation would come from outside forces such as U.S. AID funds, outspoken college students that came to study, and retirees from abroad. The societies formed to save valuable historic sites, such as the Brimstone Hill fortification, would hopefully expand their missions to save the natural environment.

The next day we left the roadstead at Charlestown, Nevis and set sail for Antigua, hoping to make it there in time for the last of the annual Race Week festivities.

Race Week

✝✝✝✝✝

Antigua to Guadeloupe

B y now Scott was very tired of the seasickness that continued
to plague him, and he returned to a more stable environment.
Burr joined the crew and brought with him a wealth of
knowledge on seabirds. We departed Nevis for what promised to be
our last major windward leg of this voyage. All the cruising guides
claimed that after Antigua, our next destination, the ensuing route
southward would put the wind on our beam. In sailing parlance, they
call the southward voyages from Antigua sleigh rides. But first, we had
to reach Antigua.

REDONDA

One cruising guide referred to this leg as ". . . one of the longest
40 miles you have ever done." With this admonition in mind, we
opted to sail for Redonda Island as an intermediate way point and
possible overnight anchorage. Redonda is an uninhabited rock about
1,000 feet high and one mile long. Its sheer walls drop sharply into
the sea with dramatic cliffs and rock falls. The guide stated that the

SATELLITE NAVIGATION

Long before the Chinese discovered the magnetic compass, Pacific islanders were using celestial navigation to find their way in the open ocean between far-flung islands. Europeans still had not ventured beyond coastal sailing within eyesight of huge continents, while Polynesians and Micronesians were finding tiny landfalls hundreds of miles away. Unfortunately, the navigational accomplishments of these islanders were handed down by word of mouth and through long apprenticeships, while western civilization carefully documented its progress and inevitably became more advanced. Now the star charts that enabled the islanders to practice celestial navigation hundreds of years before the Europeans have become museum relics and western civilization has created its own stars—satellites.

To pinpoint its Polaris submarines, the Navy launched six satellites in the 1960s which are now usable by the private sailor in a system called Transit. These six satellites spin around in north-south polar orbits less than 700 miles above the earth. From time to time, individual satellites are replaced as they drift out of orbit, but there are always a sufficient number of satellites visible to the antenna of a small sailboat to guarantee a position fix every few hours. This is a vast improvement over the traditional noon sun sight or the pre-dawn and post-dusk star sights on cloudless days with a sextant. In the 1990s, the Navy expects to launch 18 satellites, called GPS, which will guarantee sights on a continuous basis without having to wait for a satellite to come over the horizon as with the current SatNav system.

The Transit system works in the following way. Each satellite knows exactly where it is from ground signals sent to it by a master control center which measures the satellite orbits. This position information is beamed back down to any receiver tuned to the satellite's transmission. As the satellite passes overhead, the frequency of the transmission changes in the same way a train whistle's pitch shifts as the train approaches or moves away from a listener. This shift can be translated into a measure of satellite distance from the receiver. A shipborn computer, attached to the SatNav receiver, combines the satellite position information with a measurement of the frequency shift at several points in the overhead passage. With the known satellite position, the distances to the satellite, and a little geometry, the computer provides the ship's position to within tens of meters. This is much better than the normal one to two mile accuracy that can be expected from sun sights with a sextant on board a pitching sailboat, and, more importantly, the signals can be received in any kind of weather, day or night.

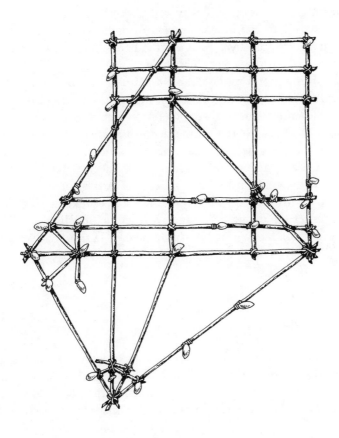

island had a post office so that sailors with a philatelic interest could obtain a rare Redonda postmark. As it turned out, the post office, perched on a cliff, had been abandoned some time ago. Maybe they couldn't find a mountain goat to act as a postmaster.

We approached Redonda around dusk and began searching for the small area noted on the charts as an "anchorage." After making several passes to convince ourselves that we were where we were supposed to be, we decided that this was no place to anchor. Fifty feet from a sheer cliff and the pounding surf, the water depth was 45 feet. At that point, I would have had so much anchor line out that I would have been nervous about dragging the anchor and swinging in too close to shore, and checking the anchor every few minutes would have resulted in a sleepless night. As long as I was going to be "on duty" all night, I thought it wiser to continue sailing for Antigua. They say that the most serious dangers faced by a boat are the hard edges around the water. Redonda looked like a very hard edge.

The evening and night sailing towards Antigua were very calm and restful under a beautiful starry night sky. Our course took us around the entire length of Monserrat which was lit up with little pinpricks of lights. At the southern tip of the island we were forced to turn on the engine briefly to make it around the bottom of this elongated island and point ourselves toward Antigua. I was losing patience with windward work, preferring to turn on the "iron sail" and get on with the trip. The engine was a good excuse to charge the batteries after an all-night passage with navigation lights, the stereo, and the care and feeding of Mr. Sulu, the ever faithful SatNav navigator.

ANTIGUA

The next day we had perfect sailing conditions closing in on Antigua. Our rust colored barn door sails were wide open to catch the beam winds all the way to the south coast of the island. However, in the last few miles before English Harbour, I made my first could-have-been-serious navigational error. I misjudged our position with respect to the harbor and motored into a large area of reefs. Fortunately, the seas were fairly calm, and the sun was still high enough to be able to see the underwater danger. I positioned myself in the bow while the crew steered to my hand signals. *Sabra*'s shallow, four-foot draft saved

the day. We never encountered anything shallower than seven feet and
we made a smooth although unorthodox entrance to English Harbour,
Antigua at around dusk.

Our arrival coincided with Antigua Race Week, a world–class

Race Week in Antigua.

racing regatta signalling the end of the Caribbean winter sailing season. Everyone who is anyone in the Eastern Caribbean sailing circuit comes to Race Week to compete and whoop it up. The locale is without question a perfect venue for sailing, racing, and partying.

English Harbour itself is a national park containing an ongoing restoration of the Nelson Dockyards. This is the most notable historic preservation of an 18th-century dockyard and the premiere historic preservation site in the Eastern Caribbean.

The Canadian government had recently become involved in the coordination of the restoration work as part of an aid program to Antigua. Canada was providing funds not only for the restoration but also for Antigua's general environmental planning.

The harbor is naturally well protected from the trade winds and Atlantic swells. It also boasts an extensive array of fortifications on the nearby headlands. It's no wonder Admiral Nelson chose this as his naval base in the region. It's also no wonder that the modern-day racing fleet chose this site for the final celebration of the sailing season.

The racing fleet of today compares to Nelson's fleet as a Trident nuclear submarine compares to a dugout canoe. We were anchored among some of the world's most awesome racing machines. Fifty feet from our anchorage was last year's round-the-world Whitbread racer, *Drum,* owned by Simon Le Bon of the rock group Duran Duran. *Credit Agricole I,* winner of the 1982 single-handed, round-the-world BOC Challenge, drifted by us looking for an anchoring spot. *Colt International, Kialoa, Shibumi,* and many other famous maxi racers were anchored all around us. *Sabra* looked like a poorly equipped dinghy in comparison to these 60- to 90-foot all-out racers.

Complementing the array of magnificent boats were the beautiful racing crews from all over the world. Bikinis, healthy suntanned bodies, and the intriguing accents of foreign languages were everywhere. It was a world-class happening!

At one point during our stay, we decided to shift our anchorage and pick up some fuel and water at the dock. The dock had room for only one boat at a time and was frequently without power to operate the fuel and water pumps. So naturally there was always a line of boats waiting to tie up. When our turn came and we were in our final maneuvers toward the fuel dock, one of the 60-plus-foot maxi racers named *Speedy Gonzales* came up alongside demanding to raft up to us. The French captain was quite determined to cut short his wait in line by tying up to us at the dock. I tried to explain to him how ludicrous

The French celebrate Race Week in Antigua with their own
distinctive burgee.

it was for such a large boat to raft up to the much smaller *Sabra*. I
finally had to ignore him but not before he tried to cut me off on my
approach to the dock. Fortunately, his size made him less maneuverable
than *Sabra*.

On a more pleasant note, I had the privilege of meeting the one
and only Donald Street. Don has written several ocean cruising books
and a multivolume set of cruising guides to the Caribbean. He is also
known for publishing a set of navigational charts of the area, and a
boat insurance business. He sails *Iolaire,* a famous 80-year old wooden
yawl, on which he has poked into every nook and cranny in the

Race Week "winner."

Caribbean. When we met, Don was on his back scraping caulking out of the seams of his dry-docked boat. He was muttering something about having been sold a bad batch of sealing compound.

At our anchoring spot in English Harbour we also met Tim and Pauline on their 24-foot wooden *Curlew*. During the cruising class races of Race Week, *Curlew,* an 1898 gaff-rigged cutter, came in second overall in a fleet of much newer and very high-tech machines. In fact, *Curlew* was beaten only by *Sur,* an Argentinian cruiser that looked much more like an all-out racer than a cruiser. It was a testament to Tim and Pauline's teamwork and sailing ability that they were able to do so well with a 90-year old boat. They have been living aboard and sailing for 20 years, and they haven't written a book about it! The next morning at dawn we saw them quietly and without fanfare gliding out of the harbor under sail in their engineless boat. It was a rewarding sight in contrast to the mega-dollar racing machines all around us.

ST. JOHN'S, ANTIGUA

The next day we took a bus to St. John's, the capital of Antigua, to make a few contacts regarding the island's environmental issues. We met Desmond Nicholson, who operates the only museum on the island and which showcases both the historic and natural features of the Antigua-Barbuda independent island nation. Nicholson was very concerned about beach and mangrove destruction due to continued resort development. He claimed that there were sufficient laws on the books to protect the environment, but that the laws weren't enforced. As an example, he cited one case where an historic site was designated by the government and then a government official, previously involved in the designation, proceeded to remove the stones of the historic building for his own private construction project. Desmond claimed that environmental awareness in the government was very low, and the officials were very ineffective. The one bright hope was funding from Canadians for parklands associated with their planned resort developments. The Canadians appeared to have substantial development investments in the Caribbean.

Desmond was very interested in environmental education material for his museum. He hoped to set up special exhibits, once he talked someone into supplying the materials, for such subjects as sea turtle protection, mangrove forest preservation, and anything on indigenous endangered species.

Our second contact in St. John's was John Fuller, an attorney and avid protector of sea turtles. John qualifies as one of those rare and unforgettable characters. Our introduction to John started when I asked him over the telephone where his office was located. His reply was, "Just ask anyone when you get in town." Sure enough, all the people we asked as we approached his office knew John's whereabouts. John's father and older brother are doctors on the island and the family is universally respected in Antigua.

We didn't realize it at the time, but we had run across John a few days earlier while reading an official tourist guide for Antigua and Barbuda which included an article by John Fuller entitled "The Sailor and the Sea Turtle." The article introduced the reader to Antigua's sea turtles and what sailors can do to protect these endangered species. It was the first time we had seen an environmental conservation message in a tourist brochure.

When we finally met, John hustled us off to his Land Rover for a luncheon meeting at a nearby private island resort. His car wouldn't start, but he didn't hesitate to stop the busy lunch hour downtown traffic to get a jump start from a passerby. He seemed to know everyone and everyone knew him so it was easy enough to flag down the first car and ask the occupant to stop in the middle of the one-lane street to get his car going.

When we were finally underway, John realized that we were late for the ferry so he got on the car's VHF radio and called ahead to another of his friends, the ferryboat operator, to have the ferry wait. The other passengers must have thought we were pretty important guests to rate this special treatment.

Once at the exclusive Jumby Bay resort, we were treated to a sumptuous buffet lunch in an extraordinarily beautiful setting. It was truly the Caribbean as it is pictured in travel brochures and novels. The setting reminded me of the hotel in the novel *Don't Stop the Carnival* by Herman Wouk. Joining us for lunch were Tom Mullen, a New Hampshire resort developer who was about to break ground on a project in Antigua, and his two assistants. They were at Jumby Bay to get ideas.

During lunch, two of the Jumby Bay managers came over to say hello to John and welcome us. Upon hearing of our interest in sea turtles they told us how interested their guests were in the sea turtle nesting beach on their property. John had been instrumental in having the Jumby Bay development take extra precautions to protect this important hawksbill nesting area. Tom was pleased to hear that the guests were showing an interest in the environment and that the nesting beach was actually a marketing advantage for the resort. He later asked me to make recommendations on environmental safeguards for his development. We exchanged business cards and promised to follow up.

It occurred to me that one of the best ways to make any headway in protecting the environment of these sensitive islands is to work with the developers. Since they are potentially the destroyers of the environment, enlisting their help is crucial. Their financial investments provide them with enormous clout. Leveraging environmental considerations through their clout may be much more effective than trying to enlist the help of a lethargic, under-funded government, or the few non-government organizations interested in the environment.

After our luncheon, Tom Mullen took us on a tour of his future beach resort development in Falmouth Harbor. He was eager to have advice regarding environmental conservation of his site. We noticed, after a brief tour of the area, the unusual amount of plastic debris washing up on his beach. The beach was facing the Atlantic, and we wondered whether the debris had originated locally or in Europe. Half kiddingly, we suggested to Tom that he could set up a plastic debris monitoring station at his future resort, using the guests to characterize and quantify the debris as it washed in daily. Such a project would add valuable scientific data while at the same time keep the beaches clean.

Another issue that came up in our conversation with John Fuller was CITES. John felt that this convention to control international trade in endangered species such as sea turtles and black coral was largely irrelevant in Antigua. Antigua is not a signatory of CITES and he saw no need to pressure the government in this direction. To him, the issues of mangrove and beach destruction were far more important than international trade in turtle products.

We learned from Desmond Nicholson that John Fuller was known to buy live sea turtles from local fishermen and then release them. In this way, he helps the fishermen earn their traditional living while saving the sea turtles. Each turtle costs him $200 to $300. He has bought some turtles several times but obviously feels that the price is worth their freedom.

GUADELOUPE

The next day, we left English Harbour at dawn for the largest of the lesser Antilles, the French island of Guadeloupe. We had a pleasant sail over the entire 40-mile route. The engine was used briefly at dusk as we made for the harbor of Deshaies before nightfall. We anchored in this quiet little harbor amid four other cruising sailboats and dinghied for shore and the gendarmerie.

Peaceful anchorage in Guadeloupe.

The gendarmes were singularly disinterested in our foreign status
and told us to check with customs in the morning. As it turned out,
the next day was Saturday and we were unable to locate the customs
official. The same was true for Sunday. Finally, on Monday morning,
after touring half the island, we were cleared to enter the French
territory of Guadeloupe.

It was at about this time in my leisure reading of a spy thriller
about Mossad, the Israeli counterpart of the CIA, that I felt like
suggesting that the Mossad use a sailboat to move agents in and out
of countries. It would avoid all that expense in buying passports or
forging paperwork. With a sailboat you just drop anchor and row
ashore. Nobody pays any attention and you have to go to extraordinary lengths, of your own initiative, to get official clearance.

We spent Saturday and Sunday in a rental car touring the island's
national park system, including a rain forest and a volcano. About 20
percent of the island has been designated as a national park, complete
with interpretive trails and information booths. Unfortunately, everything was in French, but then most U.S. park literature and signposts
are in English. The amazing thing to us was that so much of the island
had been set aside as parkland. This environmental awareness was in
sharp contrast to the documented evidence that the government was
not taking enforcement measures to curb the taking of endangered sea
turtles. Sea turtle jewelry, stuffed turtles, and sea turtle food products
were openly sold in Guadeloupe and also shipped to France for sale.
In fact, the official government visitor's guide listed turtle on the menu
of one of their recommended restaurants. In the section on where to
eat, the tourist guide stated, "Now with your appetite well-whetted,
what shall you choose? Broiled langouste or lobster? Rice and squid?
Rice and conch? You may decide on a simple turtle steak . . ."

During our travels throughout the island, it finally sank in how
expensive taxis, food, and rental cars are. Guadeloupe wasn't the only
island that we found expensive, but we were struck by the prices for
what were essentially tourist items in contrast to the obviously low
economic status of the residents. We decided that the next time we
took a trip of this nature we would lay out all our clothes in one
bundle and our money in another, then halve the amount of clothing
and double the amount of money before departing. By the time the
trip was over we expected to be talking of cutting the clothing to a
quarter and quadrupling the funds.

The language barrier, particularly in the French islands, was both amusing and a hassle. For example, when I asked for coffee I got this blank stare from the waitress. However, if I changed the pronunciation slightly to "cafe", I got an immediate "ah, cafe." They have a very narrow tolerance for mispronunciation. I never figured out how best to pronounce "operator" when I used the telephone. I thought "operator" was an international word, but apparently in Guadeloupe the word doesn't exist.

An amusing thing in Guadeloupe and Antigua were the public bus systems. The buses operated as private vehicles with standard route and fare structures. Each bus was individually decorated to the driver's particular tastes, and all have elaborate tape deck sound systems blaring the driver's preference in music. You could not take a quiet ride, read, or talk to your companion while on a bus. It was like being in the front row of a loud rock concert.

The drivers did quite a bit of hustling for business. We were about to board a bus when someone offered us a quicker ride to our destination for the same fare. As it turned out, we were simply hustled off one bus and onto another. The driver of the first bus was quite angry at having lost paying customers to a competitor.

On one of our rides in Guadeloupe, we took an early morning run which also doubled as a school bus route. The interesting thing about this ride was the number of kids the driver was able to cram aboard. Very young children were hanging all over the bus including halfway out the open door. They must not have a insurance problem on Guadeloupe. I can't imagine a similar situation in the liability conscious U.S.

ILES DES SAINTES

Toward the end of our stay in Guadeloupe we took a tour of the Iles des Saintes, a small group of islands about eight miles off the southern coast. The main community on these islands is on Terre I'en Haut, a very small picturesque French community. Unlike the main island, there had been no sugar plantations on these small islands, and therefore no slaves. As a result, the current inhabitants are mostly of Breton descent. Quite a few tourists visit these small islands and we found considerable quantities of tortoiseshell and black coral products for sale, including stuffed hawksbill heads on pedestals.

Turtle head for sale in Guadeloupe.

While waiting for the ferry to take us to the island, I had photographed a small group of gendarmes in the parking lot. Afterwards, one of them came over and said something in French that sounded like "Why were you taking our picture?" I told him I didn't speak French, and he shrugged and walked back to his companions. I wonder what he would have thought if he knew that I was photographing the police to record the fact that all the police I encountered in Guadeloupe were white in spite of the fact that the population appeared to be over 90 percent black. The same was true in St. Martin.

On the whole we found Guadeloupe to be environmentally conscious despite the turtle trade. In a 1984 report, Peter Pritchard of the

Picturesque harbor on Iles des Saintes.

Florida Audubon Society suggested that the poor record for enforcing regulations regarding sea turtles stems from political and racial sensitivities: "While ostensibly part of France, the French Antillean territories are, to all intents and purposes, colonial territories operating in a world which looks with increasing disfavor upon colonialism. The French have, fairly successfully, limited any thoughts of 'independence' by a combination of extremely substantial economic subsidy with a policy of avoiding heavy-handed enforcement of locally unpopular regulations such as those that pertain to sea turtle conservation."

We found almost no litter in the towns. Garbage cans and billboards carried messages asking the public to keep Guadeloupe beautiful. There was a sign in the tourism office regarding the protection of wild animals and quite a few signs leading to the vast amount of parkland on the island. In Basse Terre, the capital of Guadeloupe, we found no black coral or tortoiseshell products. However, Basse Terre is not a popular tourist town.

How were we to reconcile the fact that on most of the Caribbean islands we had visited it was said to be politically difficult to designate parkland, yet in Guadeloupe 20 percent of the land is in fact national parkland? On the other hand, commerce in tortoiseshell and other endangered turtle products as well as black coral was quite common and apparently not opposed by the Guadeloupe government in spite of France's participation in CITES and the existence of local laws protecting sea turtles. There were no neat answers to such paradoxes.

I had one last amusing incident the afternoon before our departure. While the crew was out exploring a nearby coral reef and I was absorbed in my spy book, I heard someone calling, *"Sabra, Sabra,"* in

Street musicians in Guadeloupe.

a decidedly French accent. I climbed out of my berth and into the cockpit where I was greeted by a middle-aged gentleman rowing a dinghy with two good-looking, topless young ladies. They didn't seem to speak English, not that it mattered, and he asked me if I would take them to Martinique. As Martinique was in the wrong direction, I declined the invitation. I watched the trio approach the other three boats in the anchorage. Apparently nobody gave them a lift, and the ladies were last seen putting on their tops and heading for town.

During Columbus' first voyage he kept hearing reports of an island called Matinino (the island of Martinique). In his log he wrote: "The indian told me of the island of Matinino, further to the east of Caribe, and said that it was inhabited only by women. . . ." Unfortunately, neither the *Niña* nor *Sabra* got a chance to check out this legend.

Esther, a derelict looking ship out of Kaoshung, Taiwan, gave us a start when she tailed us for a while before passing within 100 feet. For a rust bucket, she was bristling with very mysterious electronic antennae.

From Guadeloupe, *Sabra* made a U-turn and headed northwest with the winds abeam. We had finally turned the elusive "corner." All that beating and bashing to windward would now be a distant memory. We were getting ready for the return trip, with a stop in Cuba en route.

Turning the Corner

† † † † † †

Guadeloupe to Key West

A s we left the French island of Guadeloupe, *Sabra*'s voyage took on a decidedly different flavor. We were now headed back— we had reached the southernmost point on our Caribbean odyssey. Although we still had more than 2,500 adventurous miles ahead of us, as well as the unique opportunity of sailing into Havana, Cuba, the voyage now had the flavor of a homeward passage.

GUADELOUPE TO KEY WEST

During the first part of the return trip, *Sabra* retraced her outward track via St. Barts, St. Martin, and the Virgin Islands. From the Virgin Islands our track took us along the north coast of Puerto Rico and Hispaniola, with a brief but exciting overnight stop at Great Inagua in the Bahamas. After Great Inagua, we made a 500-mile trade-wind sprint to Key West along Cuba's north coast, threading our way through the narrow straits between Cuba and the Great Bahama Bank. From Key West we headed south again for 90 miles, and once again across the Gulf Stream, to Havana. After Havana, we planned a lei-

132

surely northward passage along the east coast to Chesapeake Bay.

As we started retracing our steps from Guadeloupe, I found myself looking forward to the Virgin Islands. In my limited opinion you don't have to go further south than the American and British Virgins to experience the magic paradise of the Caribbean. As a matter of fact the paradise becomes a little more bittersweet as you move southward. The wide separation between the haves and have-nots becomes more evident, especially when measured between visiting yachtsmen and the locals. Also the sun, the ocean, and the uniformity of tourist development have homogenized the region. Bob Shacochis, in his book of short stories entitled *Easy in The Islands* paints an accurate picture of Nevis as we saw it:

Each morning we would row our dinghy in from the anchorage to the public dock, busy in a slow way with stevedores and children, the dirty concrete piled with lumber and cases of glistening bottled beer, lumpy sacks of vegetables, hands of bananas, slaughtered animals, all steaming in the tropic sun. We wandered through the quayside markets and stalls, buying fruit from the hucksters and hot loaves of bread from an old woman who cooked them in a Dutch oven over an open fire. The bread was delicious, the day exalted unlike any I had ever known. And yet Nevis questioned me, burdened my heart with its children—preschool beggars with big eyes, kids growing up on the hot streets. Most of the population was poor, but not pathetically so. Some people lived in scrap shacks, but most owned small two-room wooden houses with rusted tin roofs and no plumbing. In these latitudes that's not as stricken as it sounds. The worst of it was the people couldn't get ahead no matter how hard they tried. In Nevis people had enough to carry on, sometimes a little more. Other than that they were stuck. Everybody but the merchants seemed terminally unemployed, although it was common for families to have a little garden or a piece of land in the hills where they could pick mangoes and grow sweet potatoes or tether a cow. Only the shop owners and civil servants could afford to dress the way they wanted; otherwise people wore clothes that were ill-fitting or torn, the zippers always busted, but rarely dirty. That's how it was in Nevis, my first true touch of paradise.

I might add that rowing ashore at Charlestown, Nevis always made me wonder whether the dinghy would be there upon my return. In Guadeloupe, for example, the dinghy was always there but it was often clear from the way it was retied that someone had used it while we were ashore.

This poverty also reminded me that saving endangered sea turtles is my problem, not theirs. Nevis has more pressing concerns. The focus of environmental protection should be on American developers, cruise ship operators, international airlines, tourist guide publishers, developed nations that buy the raw products, and others who can affect tourist behavior. Encouraging tourists to boycott tortoiseshell products would soon discourage the manufacture of these products.

GUADELOUPE TO ST. MARTIN

After all my frustrations over sailing against the trades, I now had my chance to head west and experience downwind sailing in the easterly trades. It was truly wonderful, which is the way sailing should be. The sails were boomed out like barn doors. *Sabra* charged forward, often surfing with the ocean swells. It's hard to explain the special exhilaration of sailing at a mere five to seven miles per hour to people accustomed to driving 50 to 70 miles per hour. The exhilaration comes not from the actual speed but from the sensation that you're just barely in control of a very, very large force. It's like downhill skiing or galloping on horseback, when you're trying to stay on the edge of controlling the force of gravity or the strength of the horse. We were finally living William F. Buckley's adage, "Gentlemen do not sail to windward."

The junk rig is particularly well suited to downwind sailing. The fully battened sails keep the sails open without having to rig preventers and poles to keep the sails open. The squarish shape of the junk sail has more effective area than a triangular sail. And most important, the balanced lug rig, with a small portion of the sail ahead of the mast, dampens the sometimes violent motion of an accidental jibe. This was the kind of sailing the Chinese had in mind when they invented the rig.

It was an overnight sail to the French Island of St. Barts and we tried to time our arrival in Gustavia, for the early morning hour. This would give us a chance to pick up some hot, fresh-from-the-oven croissants for a civilized breakfast treat. Unfortunately, the inner harbor was very crowded and the croissants weren't worth anchoring in the outer harbor and rowing all the way back to the town pier. What would have been an adventure on the outward passage was now viewed more as a hassle on the way home. We decided to continue on to St. Martin, promising ourselves a pizza and ice cream for dinner.

The harbor of Philipsburg looked surprisingly good to us after some of the towns and anchorages we'd encountered further south. It was comforting to go back to familiar surroundings with no apprehensions about the correct course to steer, the best place to anchor, or the mysterious customs and immigration procedures. Philipsburg was also a good place to fix the freshwater pump, which had sprung an annoying leak and needed a new gasket.

Watching things wear out and break is very much part of the cruising life. The sun's powerful rays, the caustic saltwater spray, and the constant and sometimes violent motion of the boat all contribute to wear and tear. There's no comparison with shore life. One doesn't walk around the house each day looking out for things that wore out the day before. Yet on the boat that's exactly what you must do for your very comfort and safety. You carefully inspect the lines, mechanical couplings, electrical connections, screws, and nuts, just to be sure that everything is as it should be. I looked at a portion of the boat every day and asked myself, "What's wrong with this picture?" And more often than I would have liked, there was something wrong with the picture.

Fortunately, I had been able to fix everything worn out or broken; sometimes I had to resort to a bit of bailing wire technology. It was a great source of pride to have thought well enough ahead to bring the right tools and supplies and to be able to do the repairs while underway. But whenever I first saw "what was wrong with this picture," there was that initial reaction of "Oh _____!" followed by a sinking feeling in the stomach.

What I wasn't able to deal with as well was the problem of discontinued models and poor quality control in the replacement parts. The gasket I needed for the freshwater pump was now a discontinued item. Instead of a $10 gasket, I was forced to buy this year's water pump for $80. What made matters worse was that the new model had different mounting holes, requiring a temporary jury rig. I had also ordered a new compass light to replace the one that had burned out.

THE CHINESE JUNK RIG

At first sight, the Chinese junk rig's unusual appearance may seem confusing and complicated to the western eye. In fact, it is extraordinarily simple, clever, and extremely easy to handle.

The lug sails have full-length battens, which lie across the width of the sails, from luff to leech, and divide the sails into panels. The top batten is the yard, which is a heavier spar than the other battens and takes the full weight of the sail. The bottom batten is the boom, which takes very little loading and therefore need be no stronger than the other battens. The head of the sail is secured to the yard, and the sail is raised from the cockpit by hauling on the halyard. The sail is held to the mast by batten parrel lines that run loosely around the mast at each batten. The luff of the sail always lies on the same side of the mast and extends forward of the mast, making it a balanced lug sail. On one tack the sail lies against the mast and is held off the mast by the battens. On the other tack, the sail hangs away from the mast and is held by the parrel lines. A multiple topping lift system—lazyjacks—passes under the boom and lies on both sides of the sail forming a cradle, which holds the sail when it is reefed or furled.

Two additional parrel lines are led back to the cockpit to control the fore and aft position of the sail. The yard parrel is used to bring the yard snugly against the mast. This is only important when the sail is reefed and has a tendency to swing aft of the mast. Similarly, a luff parrel line is used to prevent the sail from swinging too far forward of the mast and to maintain tension on the luff of the sail. Both of these lines are used to shift the position of the sail and fine tune the rig.

A single sheet system controls the aft end of the boom and the five lower battens by a system of spans (sheetlets) and blocks. This gives control over the entire leech of the sail, not just the boom, and reduces the twist of the sail. The main part of the sheet system is one long length of line that runs through blocks and forms a purchase system so that loading on the tail end is light.

The portion of the balanced lug sail forward of the mast performs an important function, contributing to the safety and comfort of this rig. When the wind and boat direction conspire to create an accidental jibe, the small portion of the sail in front of the mast actually dampens the motion of the sail and therefore slows down an otherwise violent motion. Both intentional and accidental jibing become much less hair-raising.

The key features of the Chinese junk rig are ease of handling, simplicity of use, and self-reefing and furling for the shorthanded crew. These features may not contribute to an America's Cup contender, but they do add up to safe, relaxed, and efficient cruising with an emphasis on comfortable passagemaking.

Fortunately, I ordered two so that I would have a spare and, as it turned out, one was defective. It's depressing to think that you have to order twice the number of replacements in order to compensate for poor quality control.

A little later in the return trip, I broke valve springs on both of the engine's cylinder heads. This required some machine shop assistance in St. Thomas. The mechanic could find no replacement valves for my Volvo so he proceeded to hammer the bent valve stem straight—a very unorthodox procedure for such a precision part. But he gave me his famous five minute or five mile guarantee, whichever came first, and sent me on my way. The engine is still working. That's one way to get around the high cost of Volvo replacement parts.

That night in St. Martin, we repeated the wonderful pizza and ice cream experience we had on our way out. They were just as good the second time around. At home I took such items for granted but out here they took on a special significance. We had talked about these treats all the way from St. Barts to St. Martin and they helped overcome the disappointment of missing out on the croissants.

Reflecting on the simple pleasure of a pizza made me think of other things that I had taken for granted. For example, I was beginning to forget what it was like to have a front door to my home to simply walk through. For several months, I'd had to scamper down the side of my home into a bobbing dinghy with my shoes in my knapsack. Then on the return trip I had to carefully off-load grocery bags or other items with one hand while holding myself and the dinghy alongside *Sabra*. Then hoist myself up the four-foot side of the boat while clutching the lifeline and the dinghy line. All this became very tricky with a swell running through the anchorage. A front door would really seem strange when I returned.

ST. MARTIN TO VIRGIN GORDA

For the first time in over 2,000 miles of sailing we had to take steps to slow *Sabra* down. We had planned an overnight passage to Virgin Gorda and the Bitter End Yacht Club. However, sailing conditions were so perfect that by 2 A.M. we were very close to the coral reefs that protect the eastern entrance to Virgin Gorda Sound. We had to reef the sails and slow the boat to a creep in order to negotiate the entrance in daylight. I was still amazed at the difference between upwind and downwind cruising. It's like two different sports.

By 7 A.M. we were comfortably seated on the beachfront patio of the Bitter End Yacht Club feeling very smug about our sailing accomplishments and enjoying a delicious breakfast buffet. Two couples seated next to us asked how we liked the hotel. We told them that we were not guests, just sailors passing through. The men were impressed that only minutes ago we had arrived from St. Martin and that we were on an extensive cruise of the Caribbean. One of the couples

A tired voyager takes a break on *Sabra*'s deck.

was on their honeymoon and the man said that he was hoping that someday he could take a similar cruise. He asked lots of questions while his wife looked on with increasing nervousness.

As I talked to these people, and as I watched the day sailors and Virgin Island charterers, I felt very proud of my voyage and the accomplishments of *Sabra* and her crew. I also had some mixed feelings, sitting at this posh hotel, about my willingness and eagerness to take advantage of the good life in spite of feeling good at having achieved something special without all the normal amenities. I was trying to convince myself that it's OK to feel admirable for being able to live without creature comforts, and at times in discomfort, but that it's no sin to come back to appreciate and want those comforts.

THE HARD EDGES OF GREAT INAGUA

After removing the head of the Volvo diesel for the third time on this trip to replace a valve spring, we departed St. Thomas for Key West. I was getting to be quite an engine mechanic by this time. I had also decided that in my next life I was coming back as a Volvo parts distributor to really make some big bucks.

Ellison, who had started the trip from Washington, D.C., was now back aboard along with his brother Robert to help on the passage to Key West. To give the crew a break in what was to be a 10-day, 1,000-mile passage, we decided to stop in Great Inagua. This is the third largest of the Bahama islands and the most southerly, lying approximately on our route to Key West. Great Inagua almost proved to be the end of *Sabra*'s voyage.

The first few days out of St. Thomas were marked by annoying calms and rain. Apparently a large weather system was sitting over the area and blanking out the normal trade winds. Finally, the trades returned with a gusto and we made for Matthew Town.

We had a difficult time finding the entrance to the newly dredged 200-by-200-foot basin, which was Inagua's idea of a harbor. My intuition told me to bag this stopover and continue on to Key West. We didn't need any provisions, not that any were available in this remote island. However, Robert was very seasick and had begun to hallucinate from the Scopolamine patches behind his ear. He wanted off the boat. He was planning on catching the weekly flight to Nassau and Miami. So, against better judgment, we entered the 30-foot-wide channel and dropped our anchor in the middle of what looked like a large bathtub.

We were the only boat in the "anchorage" aside from a small beat-up trawler tied to the pier. We tied a stern line to the pier to keep the boat from swinging into the entrance channel and went to the police barracks to check on clearance procedures. Naturally, customs was closed for the day. They're always closed when *Sabra* arrives.

We then walked into town for dinner. Outside the only open restaurant and bar we were stopped by a very large, black, off-duty immigration official. He wanted to know if we were cleared. We told

Reality for this crew member is seasickness.

him of our conversation with the police and our intention to get cleared as soon as customs opened in the morning. He was not sympathetic to our situation and said, "You should have stayed on the boat until we were contacted. You are now illegal aliens on Bahamian soil." I asked him what we should do now and he said it would cost "overtime" to straighten this matter out. He instructed us to have dinner while he worked out the details of our predicament. This was going to be a very expensive dinner.

On every other island we had visited, a closed customs office simply meant that you should conduct business as usual, in other words spend money and enjoy yourself, and return for clearance when customs opened.

About an hour later, as we were waiting for our ice cream after a very good fish 'n' chips dinner, the officer returned and told us to get back to the boat quickly because a storm was coming. We rushed back and to our horror found that the anchor had dragged and *Sabra* was now bashing herself against the concrete pier with that sickening crunching sound of fiberglass against concrete. By now the wind had begun to scream in the rigging and trees, large swells were coming into the basin, and the rain was flying horizontally. Quite a contrast to the serene bathtub scene a few hours earlier.

I couldn't believe how quickly the weather had changed and how dangerous the situation had become. I had visions of broken fiberglass all along the length of the boat. The hull would break long before it scratched the concrete. I had once sailed with a concrete foundations contractor who was fond of saying, "Concrete is final!"

Without much thought of personal safety, and ignoring the dinghy, I jumped down three feet from the pier to *Sabra*'s deck and ran below to start the engine. At the time I didn't know whether the anchor chain was still connected to the boat. I screamed to the crew to release the stern line which was still connected to the pier. As soon as I saw the line free I gave the engine full power in a desperate attempt to get clear of the pier. We slowly and agonizingly inched ourselves away from the unyielding concrete.

After undoing the line, Ellison made a spectacular leap off the pier onto the deck. It was an Olympic performance for someone who had been behind a Washington, D.C. desk for the past 20 years. Together we proceeded to execute a delicate series of engine and tiller maneuvers resulting in figure eights in front of the inlet and the oncoming swells. We would nose the bow into the wind attempting to keep *Sabra* in mid-basin. As the wind and swells knocked us to one side we would power back to the center, cut the power to avoid getting too close to the entrance, and then be pushed to the other side. We repeated this maneuver for about 45 minutes waiting for the wind to abate.

We were too busy tending the throttle and tiller to wonder how this drama would end. We briefly thought about reanchoring but there was no room in the basin to get close enough to pick up the anchor, which by now we had determined to be still attached to the boat, without being smashed against the pier. We were also without the dinghy, so setting another anchor was out of the question. Our mouths were very, very dry. I wondered how much of an adrenalin supply the body has. How long could we keep up the intense concentration it took to keep a 32-foot boat from smacking into the hard edges surrounding a 200-foot square basin awash in swells and howling wind?

The storm finally died down as quickly as it had come up, and once again we were in a quiet bathtub. We picked up the anchor, reset it, and slapped each other on the back for a job well done. It didn't take any words to congratulate each other for literally having saved *Sabra*.

We officially cleared into the Bahamas the next day with the same immigration official we had met the night before. He advised us that he would come by later for his "overtime" fee. However, by then we were gone, not wanting to chance another surprise storm.

To our amazement, the damage sustained by *Sabra* was quite minimal—a few scratches here and there. We owed our good fortune to having arrived just as *Sabra* first encountered the pier and to the fact that there were a few old wooden boards nailed to the pier to cushion boat hulls. The only loss was another dinghy oar. We had been very, very lucky.

ALONG CUBA'S NORTH COAST

From Great Inagua we headed west northwest for 500 miles along Cuba's north coast towards Key West. Most of this passage was made within 50 miles of Cuba. Our closest point to the island was a mere seven miles. We were a bit nervous about intruding on Cuba's territorial waters, but the shoals of the Great Bahama Bank on the other side of the passage made us even more nervous. We were truly between a rock and a hard place. I was later told by a State Department geographer that in narrow navigable channels vessels have "rights of innocent passage" that supersede the normal territorial limits of a nation.

The night sailing along the island was particularly interesting because we could see the shore lights on Cuba. It was also a bit tense because of all the commercial shipping that squeezes into this narrow channel between the Bahamas and Cuba. Night sailing is much more interesting and challenging than day sailing. For one thing, you're hurling the boat into black nothingness on the faith of your navigation and the chart. You're absolutely blind. The only things to see are the lights of other ships and those have to be studied carefully to be sure they're not aimed at you on a collision course. Chances are that you're too small to be seen by commercial ships, so its your responsibility to stay out of their way.

We contacted several freighters and tankers to be sure they saw us on their radar screens. Most were very courteous and acknowledged our radar image. Some didn't bother to answer and I wondered if anyone was on the bridge or was the ship simply on autopilot, unmindful of small boats in the vicinity.

During the long black night watches, with *Sabra* sailing herself so close to Cuba under control of Pierre, the wind vane, I thought how easy it would be to think of myself as a citizen of the world. My allegiances would be to nature and its land forms. The limitless seas, the absoluteness of stars and sun, and the ever changing wind patterns would be my only realities. The enemy wouldn't be the government of Cuba, it would be carelessness and disregard for nature.

These thoughts came about as a result of the bits and pieces of far-off newscasts we were receiving on the Iran-Contra hearings. The contrast of our isolation in the vast ocean to the shenanigans of Ollie North made it easy to be contemplative and philosophical.

No Problemas

✝✝✝✝✝

Key West to Havana and Back

A fter a 1,000-mile, 10-day journey from St. Thomas, Virgin Islands, to Key West, Florida, *Sabra* tied up at Lands End Marina for less than 24 hours before setting off on an exciting voyage to Cuba. Since the early planning stages of this marine conservation project, I had been struck by the enormous physical presence and the enigma of Cuba in the Caribbean Basin. Because the island is by far the largest of the Greater Antilles, there would be no way to get a true feeling for the marine conservation issues of this region without making contact with Cuba. Cuba is a regular consumer of endangered sea turtle meat and a major exporter of tortoiseshell products to Japan. In the past few years, though, several positive environmental conservation stories had emerged from the island, including work to save the extremely rare ivory-billed woodpecker, and programs for the preservation of endangered crocodiles. I was convinced that Cuba would be an environmental and sailing highlight of *Sabra*'s marine conservation voyage. I was right.

GAINING PERMISSION

The first obstacle to visiting Cuba is the travel restriction imposed by the U.S. government. After some digging through the Washington, D.C. telephone directories and numerous calls to federal agencies, I was surprised to learn that the Foreign Assets Control office of the Treasury Department grants (or denies) permission to visit Cuba. It appears that the travel restriction is not about *visiting* the island, but on spending U.S. dollars there. You can't buy a cup of Cuban coffee without Treasury's approval.

I sent a letter explaining *Sabra*'s project and our interest in visiting with the Cubans to the office of Foreign Assets Control. Before they had a chance to respond, I made a follow-up call only to learn that the request was about to be denied because I hadn't demonstrated sufficient reason for setting foot on the island. After several more telephone calls and letters which emphasized Cuba's importance and uniqueness for Caribbean conservation, we received permission for *Sabra* and her crew to sail to Cuba.

Our next step was to contact the Cuban Interest Section in Washington, D.C. Without full diplomatic relations, both countries operate under "interest sections" in third-country embassies. Cuba's office is in the Czechoslovakian Embassy. Negotiations took place between Cuban representatives and the Center for Marine Conservation while *Sabra* sailed for the Caribbean. Well received by the Cubans, our staff was told that the visit presented, *"No problemas."* These words seem to be a catch phrase in the Caribbean.

Everywhere we'd been we'd heard the standard answer: "No problem." Often times there are plenty of problems, but in this case there truly were none. As a matter of fact, the Cubans encouraged us to visit their island and hoped we could time our visit to coincide with a major marine conference in early June.

Having received the necessary permission from both sides, *Sabra* cut short her planned tour of the Windward Islands—Dominica, St. Lucia, St. Vincent, and Grenada—in order to be in Cuba for the marine conference. It would give us a perfect opportunity to meet the people connected with marine conservation.

FIRST ENCOUNTER

Michael flew down from Washington to join me on this momentous leg of the voyage. Before leaving Key West, we tied up to a fuel dock to top off the tank. The operator was a bit disgruntled over having had his lunch hour cut short, especially for our big four-gallon purchase. However, when he found out that we were headed for Cuba, his demeanor changed abruptly as he started telling us of his visits to the island prior to the revolution. He obviously enjoyed the island and was envious of our permission to visit. We promised to look him up on our return and tell him of our experiences.

This was my third crossing of the infamous Gulf Stream. The stream in this area flows with an average velocity of two to three knots towards the east. Therefore, on a southbound passage we set a course for about 50 miles to the west of where we planned to end up. "Mr. Sulu," our SatNav navigator, was primed for this aberration and we pushed out into the Florida Straits about midday. Soon after we left the protection of the shallow banks, the afternoon winds started piping up in opposition to the current flow, and the seas started building up and up and up. . .

By the time it was dark, the waves had achieved enormous proportions, at least in our minds. The darkness only added to their immensity. Michael, who in a previous life had been a Southern California surfer and intimately familiar with waves, estimated that their height was in the eight- to 15-foot category. The problem wasn't so much their height but the irregularity of their arrival. Not only did the waves not come in predictable and regular intervals, they also came from all directions. As we sat in the cockpit, we stared ahead into pitch-black nothingness, waiting for the next surprise wave and hoping it wouldn't be one of those oversized rogue waves you read about in sailing horror stories.

By early morning, land forms were beginning to emerge on the horizon, and in spite of our sleepless night our level of anticipation and excitement grew at seeing the forbidden shores of Cuba. I hoisted the Cuban courtesy flag in my best show of friendliness and made certain that the U.S. flag was prominently visible. About 10 miles from

Our best show of friendship, the Cuban courtesy flag.

shore, according to Mr. Sulu, we saw a Russian freighter and took several pictures with the barely visible Havana skyline in the background. No sooner had the freighter passed and we had put our cameras away when a gunboat began bearing down on us from some distance away. I told Michael to warm up his Spanish because the Cubans were coming at about 40 miles per hour in a flurry of spray and there were intimidating gun mounts fore and aft.

We dropped our sails and tried to raise the marina on the VHF radio, hoping that they were forewarned of our visit. No one responded. We were left to deal with the gunboat as best we could. As it closed the distance, I noticed two or three uniformed men and about a half dozen in T-shirts and shorts of various colors. The boat itself was a military gray color similar to our own Navy vessels. However, the colorful, nonuniform dress gave the crew somewhat of a ragtag look.

They slowed down and started shouting at us in Spanish over the roar of the engines, saying that we weren't supposed to be in this "zone." I assumed they meant Cuba's territorial waters. Michael shouted back in his best Spanish that we had permission. This exchange lasted for several minutes as each side tried to understand the other and the two boats wallowed in the swells. Finally, they seemed to understand that we did have permission as well as Cuban visas and were on our way to Marina Hemingway on the outskirts of Havana. We were then escorted towards the entrance channel. Although we raised our sails and started the engine to gain speed, the gunboat would lurch ahead at 40 mph and then stop to wait for us to catch up. We must have made an interesting picture—a Chinese junk-rigged sailboat trying to keep up with a high-speed Cuban gunboat. Actually, it was fortunate that the gunboat came by. Mr. Sulu knew exactly where our destination lay, but I was unwilling to charge ahead toward an unfamiliar shore simply on his say-so when I couldn't see the actual channel with my own eyes.

About one-half mile from shore a small speedboat approached and escorted us to a military outpost at the head of the channel. There we were told to tie up for what became a lengthy but very civilized six-hour clearance process. We were in Cuba!

A Cuban gun boat leads *Sabra* to the marina.

CLEARING CUSTOMS AND IMMIGRATION

The small outpost contained about six uniformed soldiers, without visible guns, in a nicely appointed two-room building on the edge of the entrance channel to Marina Hemingway. One room had a metal desk, two chairs, a filing cabinet, and photos of Fidel and Che. The other room was a combination kitchen, dining area, and sitting room, complete with TV, table and chairs, and a couch. At first we stood around while they made some calls to alert immigration officials. They offered us coffee; we watched a little TV; we walked around the yard and pier; and were politely asked not to take pictures. After about an hour of hanging around and being excited about being in Cuba, our sleepless night caught up with us and we returned to the boat for a nap in the cockpit.

We were sound asleep about two hours later when one of the officers awoke us with some long unintelligible Spanish question ending in "Volvo Penta," the only two words I understood. As additional information on the boat was needed, we returned to the office where two officers proceeded to fill out many, many forms by hand. Some had to be filled out in quintuplicate, without the aid of carbon paper. The immigration folks still hadn't come, but the military types had decided to start the boat clearance process.

Negotiate our entry with immigration officials. *No Problemas*!

We were told to motor about a mile down the channel to Marina Hemingway and our slip. After a perfunctory search, we shook hands and cast off. I got the feeling that they just wanted to see the boat's interior. Hardly any of the cabinets were opened and nothing was touched by the officers. They had been very pleasant and apologized for the long delay.

At the marina we were directed to the slip by a handful of civilians and several uniformed officers. They helped us tie *Sabra* to the pier, and we followed them into a room that served as a country club sitting room. The marina is quite large and hosts deep-sea fishing tournaments. It is able to accommodate several hundred boats, but we saw only four

A country club atmosphere outside of Havana.

Cubans love their "Papa," Ernest Hemingway.

motor and two sailboats. We were apparently there between tournaments and the place was almost empty, but fully staffed. We were beginning to see that everyone is employed in Cuba whether work needs doing or not.

Inside, eight of us sat in rocking and easy chairs set up in a circle with a couple of folding TV tables in front of the officers. Again we filled out a multitude of multipart forms which kept being passed around from one person to another. Each person seemed to look over the form and add something or rubber stamp it. It looked like some crazy game with forms flying back and forth across the circle. In the middle of this form frenzy, a couple of waiters in white uniforms came

An empty, but fully staffed, marina.

in with trays of ice water and Cuban coffee. Everyone relaxed for a bit, and I sampled my first industrial strength Cuban coffee over a heaping bed of sugar.

Most of the forms and questions were straightforward and expected. "Where did you come from?" "Do you have any firearms aboard?" "Are you carrying any drugs?" The only unexpected question was "Do you have any pornographic materials?" I guess they still remember America's contribution to the "sin city" days of prerevolution Havana. We finally ran out of forms and turned to small talk as we sipped our coffee. Renaldo, one of the civilians attached to the marina, wanted to practice his English. We complimented everyone on the friendly atmosphere during the clearance process. They assured us that only the two governments have problems. Between the peoples of Cuba and America there are *"no problemas."* Later that day we saw a huge billboard with a cartoon character of Uncle Sam standing on the Florida peninsula and a Cuban soldier shouting across the water, "Mr. Imperialist, we are not afraid of you!"

We had a pleasant dinner at the Havana Libre Hotel overlooking the city and returned for a well deserved sleep before the marine conference the next day. It had been an exciting but exhausting, and mostly sleepless, 36 hours since Key West.

"Mr. Imperialist: We are absolutely not afraid of you!"

Skyline from the Havana Libre hotel.

THE ENVIRONMENTAL SCENE IN CUBA

Over the next three days we learned a number of interesting and potentially valuable things about Cuba's environmental and conservation activities, particularly in connection with endangered sea turtles. We were very fortunate to meet several officials of the Fisheries Ministry, including Elvira Carrillo, the *directora* of the fishing regulations office directly under the fisheries minister. We also had an opportunity to talk with Orlando Garrido, a leading bird-watcher who was the last person to see the ivory-billed woodpecker before the recent sightings, and a former member of the Cuban Academy of Sciences.

Following is a brief summary of what we learned.

First of all, the officials were very pleased that we were in Cuba and showing an interest in their programs. We were the first American environmental group to have talked to the fisheries people about marine conservation issues including sea turtles, coral, manatees, and other marine mammals.

Cuba appeared to have more people working on sea turtle conservation issues than any other Caribbean basin country. Yet, surprisingly, Cuba was not represented at the major international conferences that deal with sea turtles in this region.

In spite of an admitted decline in sea turtle populations fishermen were allowed to continue taking sea turtles, except during the nesting season. However, the officials we met hoped that this decline could be reversed by ranching or farming sea turtles. It was obvious that the Cubans did not realize how difficult it is to develop and operate sea turtle mariculture programs. There are still many unanswered questions about sea turtle biology, and these programs are still in the experimental stage.

To date Cuba has started two or three ranching operations for hawksbill and green turtles. There was about a 50 percent hatch rate, which is not too good, with all but a few of the hatchlings being returned to the sea. The few not released were kept for further research. They hoped that this type of ranching would increase the survivability of hatchling and thus increase the population. Their evidence suggested that hawksbills released in Cuban waters remain in Cuban waters to the benefit of Cuban fishermen.

The Cubans were planning to start more ranching programs as well as farming programs where a portion of the hatchlings would be retained for slaughter. Cuba exports a lot of tortoiseshell to Japan where it is turned into jewelry and cosmetic products, and sea turtle meat is commonly eaten in Cuba.

In spite of the existing and planned ranching operations, there seemed to be very little in the way of published data on hatchling success rates and other scientific aspects of these programs. Hopefully, further collaborative exchanges with scientists would yield such data or make the Cubans aware of the latest scientific protocol in developing the data.

The Cubans were hoping to attend the Western Atlantic Turtle Symposium in Puerto Rico later that year, but visas from the U.S. government were a problem. We said that we would do all we could

An endangered green sea turtle, stuffed, wrapped, and for sale in Cuba.

to help them secure permission to participate in this meeting.

Although there seemed to be no shortage of personnel in turtle programs, they were desperately short of funds for research equipment, such as tags for released turtles and calipers for taking measurements. We were told that even paper is in short supply. Bibliographies and research papers were also needed.

During the early stages of our meetings, we distributed reports, books, and papers published by the Center to explain our areas of interest and to share our information. These items were eagerly accepted by the fisheries ministry officials and in a subsequent meeting we were given a preliminary report on sea turtle operations in Cuba.

Hopefully, more reports will be forthcoming in the future. We also gave out lapel pins with the Center's marine logo, and we noticed that they proudly wore the pins the next day.

After our first meeting, they promised to introduce us to the *directora* in charge of fishing regulations and the person most influential in deciding whether Cuba will seek membership in CITES. We had come to Cuba thinking that if we could convince these officials to think about joining the Convention on International Trade in Endangered Species of Wild Flora and Fauna we would have scored a successful first encounter towards conserving sea turtles and other endangered Caribbean wildlife.

On our first day we gave our contact several items describing CITES and the 95 countries that are signatories to this convention. Then, two days later, when we finally met Elvira Carillo, the *directora,* we learned that having read our materials on CITES, she was interested in the convention and planned to send an observer to that year's meeting in Ottawa, if formally invited. We said that we would do everything possible to have the CITES secretariat send a formal invitation. If nothing else, the *directora*'s interest in CITES and a willingness to send an observer to this year's meeting was worth the trip.

One interesting aspect of our meeting with Elvira was over the recurring matter of what to wear. It was getting harder and harder to put on shoes, socks, and long pants in this sun-soaked tropical paradise. Michael and I discussed this important point of protocol the day before the promised meeting, and he even went out to buy a new *guayabera* shirt for the occasion. I had put on long khaki pants and deck shoes, but no socks, for our first meeting. But the upcoming meeting with someone only one bureaucratic level away from Fidel Castro required something better. I decided on dress slacks, regular shoes, socks, and a button-down oxford shirt. I was toying with the notion of a sports coat but that seemed insane in this heat and, of course, no one wore ties.

When I unzipped my garment bag for the first time in five months, I found that the sport coat and all my slacks were mildewed. I selected the least moldy looking pair of slacks and left the jacket behind. When we arrived for the much hoped for meeting with a high official, we were told that she was out of the city but that she would try to see us at the marina later on. We left thinking that our chances of meeting her before our scheduled departure were slim. Later on that afternoon, when we were back at the boat and in our standard barefoot uniforms of shorts and T-shirts, Elvira Carillo showed up. I quickly put on my deck shoes and we had a wonderful meeting with her. And I didn't smell of mold as I had earlier in the day. Life in the tropics can be difficult.

During our last afternoon in Cuba we met Orlando Garrido, a former member of the Cuban Academy of Sciences. Sr. Garrido is author of several Cuban field guides to birds and reptiles and was soon to be appointed to the Museum of Natural History which was expanding its collaborative research with other countries. He provided us with additional insights into the environmental scene in Cuba.

The government and the people of Cuba are very environmentally aware, probably as a result of a long running Spanish TV series called

The Directora, Dr. Elvira Carillo, makes an unannounced visit to *Sabra* and her well-dressed crew.

I interview Orlando Garrido, a former member of the Cuban
Academy of Science.

"Man and the Earth" shown nationwide some years earlier. We also
learned of a local TV conservation program that continued to keep up
the public's environmental awareness.

Cuba has established four national parks since 1962. An additional
125 parks have been proposed. When asked if park rangers were able
to enforce the hunting and wood cutting conservation restrictions in
these parks, Sr. Garrido said that one park alone was staffed with 125
police (rangers). Manpower is no problem in a socialist planned economy. You just direct 125 persons from one activity to another. Everyone literally works for the government.

When the ivory-billed woodpecker was sighted in 1986 after it

A fishing port, not quite as elegant as Marina Hemingway.

had been thought to be extinct, the government ordered a stop to logging and rerouted a highway that had been planned through the area.

We learned that there were no nongovernment environmental organizations in Cuba. As a matter of fact, there weren't even any local bird-watching or diving enthusiasts groups. Canadians, with the cooperation of Cuban officials, had recently begun organizing bird-watching expeditions for tourists.

The Cuban government was starting to recognize the need for collaborative research with other countries, and Garrido hoped the museum will fill this role.

Orlando Garrido, as well as all the other Cubans we had met in connection with environmental matters, were very encouraging about our interest in a continuing dialogue with Cuba. We were invited to return for a more in-depth tour. Apparently we had come at the right time.

CLEARING OUT

We had arranged with the marina to start the outward clearance process early the next morning. Anticipating another long session, we asked them to come by early because we had a long sail ahead of us. They really took us seriously; at 6 A.M. there was a knock on the deck, and two uniformed officers were there to process our exit. I invited them aboard but they declined, saying that their boots would scuff the deck. In no other country, including the U.S., had we ever received such consideration. Under the light of a flashlight, the whole process took only 15 minutes and there we were, half asleep and hardly ready to go.

We asked if we could stay long enough to have a shower and breakfast. They agreed and posted a guard by the boat who would later accompany us to the military outpost at the entrance channel. We ate, paid our marina bill, said our good-byes, and motored over to the outpost to drop off the military officer who had been guarding the boat. He made one last inspection of the boat, presumably to be sure we weren't taking any defectors off the island, and bid us good-bye and good sailing. We hoisted sails and prepared to do battle with the Gulf Stream for the fourth and final time on this voyage.

SOME ADDITIONAL THOUGHTS ON CUBA

The 90-mile passage back to Key West was relatively calm considering that we were crossing the Gulf Stream and close reaching against the easterly trades. We spent much of the time discussing and reflecting on our brief yet intense visit. I was particularly struck by four observations of this communist island so close to our shores.

First, the people were as friendly and happy as any you would find

Suntan maintenance is free and plentiful.

in the U.S. under similar circumstances. They didn't fit the dour, oppressed stereotype that I had had in my mind. I think the most telling evidence of this, apart from our warm reception, was the nightly congregation at lovers' lane along the Malecon. The Malecon is a wide boulevard surrounding a large part of the city along the coast. It has a short stone wall separating the ocean from the sidewalk and runs for miles. In the balmy evening hours lovers gather all along this wall. Every 30 or 50 feet a couple would be sitting, standing, or lying in every imaginable fashion while embracing and kissing. All ages were represented, and everyone exuded a clear and unmistakable sign of their happiness.

Havana needs lots of expensive street maintenance and house painting.

The second thing that struck me in touring Havana was the architectural beauty of the city. Havana is a coast city of about two million people. The city had a European ambience with narrow streets and very ornate buildings. But unlike Europe, the buildings were painted in beautifully bright pastel shades to compliment the sun, sea, and sky. Sunsets reflecting off the row of buildings along the Malecon were particularly striking. Unfortunately, the buildings were in disrepair and badly in need of new paint. A local U.N. World Health Organization official told us that quite a bit of restoration was underway by local neighborhood committees. The government provided materials and the committees provided the labor.

Cubans manage to keep an incredible number of 1940s and 1950s cars on the road.

The third observation was about how the place operated from an economic standpoint. Stores were hard to find and the few that I did see had very little on their shelves. There was a separate set of stores for the tourists which were well stocked with a strange assortment of international products as well as a few local handicrafts. You found Liquid Plumber alongside Christian Dior cosmetics and stuffed turtle heads. Anybody may shop in these stores but only U.S. dollars were accepted, thus preventing locals from shopping there unless they had come by some U.S. currency.

Similarly, we found tourist restaurants and taxis that only accepted U.S. dollars. We stopped at one "local" restaurant for a drink and light

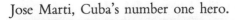

Jose Marti, Cuba's number one hero.

snack. The only items on the menu were coffee and milk. Surprisingly, there was no food. There were three waitresses and no patrons. You would have thought that the owner would have a more varied menu to attract customers and thus make more money. But here in Cuba, the restaurant was owned by the government, the waitresses and owner were paid by the government, and no one cared if there were customers or not.

The only people not working directly for the government were retirees who elected to do some contract work for the government. Sr. Garrido, the author of the bird field guides, said that he wrote these books more or less as a hobby. The government editors accepted his proposals and outlines and paid him 10 to 12 dollars per page. The government then published the books. Incidentally, we learned that novelists only got about six to eight dollars per page.

Books in Cuba are very cheap. We bought a hardcover, two-inch-thick textbook for four dollars. The bird field guides with color pictures were less than a dollar each.

The fourth observation was of the lack of visible weapons and military and police personnel. We were free to go anywhere in Havana's public areas and were allowed to rent a car for a drive through the countryside. At no time did I feel that we were restricted about taking pictures, except at the military outpost during our clearance process.

I look forward to visiting Cuba again, especially the Caribbean south coast, not only to continue our environmental conservation work but also to flesh out some of these observations. It was a marvelous, eye-opening visit.

The Conchs

✝✝✝✝✝

Key West to Palm Beach

On our return from Cuba we experienced the first truly fright-ening moment of the trip. In the predawn darkness of the Gulf Stream, Michael was at the helm and I was below catching a few winks. Michael called me topside to check out the navigation lights of a passing freighter that looked like it was on a collision course with *Sabra.* In my half awake state, I said, *"No problema,* we have plenty of sea room." But I was wrong, very wrong. Moments later the freighter's massive black hull was clearly visible in the darkness and it was bearing down on us at an alarming rate.

Because of the wind's direction and the nearness of the freighter, we had absolutely no maneuvering room under sail. Apparently the freighter's crew hadn't seen us on their radar nor had they noticed our navigation lights. I jumped below to start the engine and came back up to push the tiller over for a hard right turn away from the ship's path. By this time Michael was able to clearly see someone walking on the dark bridge of the freighter which was now less than 50 yards away. The throb of the freighter's engine and the smell of its diesel exhaust fumes filled the night air around us.

After a few anxious seconds of full power, we slowly pulled away. We began to relax a little although the adrenaline rush was still with us. There must not have been anyone on duty, or awake, on the freighter's bridge. I had called several tankers, freighters, and cruise ships on the VHF radio earlier on this trip to check on *Sabra*'s radar reflector. We were clearly visible on radar screens from at least 10 miles—if anyone cared to look. Unfortunately, it takes more than electronics to avoid collisions. Human attention is needed to interpret the electronic data, make the correct decisions, and take action. Apparently this important link was missing on this occasion.

In our anxiety over the close call, we didn't think to note the freighter's name. I would have liked to write them a letter on the subject of good seamanship.

We stopped for several days in Key West to see the sights and to contact a local conservation group active in protecting reefs, sea turtle nesting beaches, and mangrove flats, and in educating the public on the ubiquitous plastic pollution problem. One of the most recent environmental concerns in this region is the talk of oil exploration. As is so often the case, nature has put oil in some very sensitive places—the Santa Barbara Channel, the Arctic Ocean, Georges Bank . . .

Another reason for stopping in Key West was to contact the press about our story on Cuba. I was eager to share the news about this rare opportunity we had had to visit Havana. I called the *Miami Herald* and the *Key West Citizen* and got a surprisingly nonchalant response. "Gee, that's interesting but I can't come over to interview you, this is my night to wash my hair and socks." I decided to drop off my Cuba report in the hope that they would use it on a slow news day.

KEY WEST

Key West is the southernmost place in the United States. The local telephone directory describes it as "the end of the world as we know it." It goes on to say, ". . . It is a quaint conglomerate of Conch architecture, native and transplanted residents, and colorful tropical lifestyles. 'Conchs' are native residents, all others are 'Key Westers' or 'Strangers' . . . all this has led to a live-and-let-live philosophy."

I would add that quite a few of the people look like '60s hippies with long and greying hair. Young or old, many look like dropouts or rejects from the rest of society. Maybe being southernmost has a low point or drain effect. I went to a fancy hairdresser to see if they could revive my sun drenched, saltwater soaked hair. While she worked at trying to turn straw back into hair, she said that she and her husband had moved here from Carmel, California (not exactly the mainstream of the U.S.), and she had never seen a weirder group of people.

The town caters to tourists and is filled with trendy boutiques, T-shirt shops, dive shops, charter boats for fishing and sailing, and lots of eateries and watering holes. The big event in Key West is the daily gathering at Mallory Square to watch the sun set. If you're lucky, you can also see the famous and illusive "green flash" just after the sun goes under.

At Mallory Square you also get to see the local street people.

Endangered green sea turtles in a Key West headstart program.

SEA TURTLES

Six of the world's eight species of sea turtles are found in the Caribbean and southeastern U.S. All six of these species—the hawksbill, green, Kemp's ridley, loggerhead, olive ridley, and leatherback—are considered to be in danger of extinction. These sea reptiles have been safe in the oceans for 100 million years, back to the days of the dinosaurs, but now man threatens their survival.

Leatherbacks are the largest of the sea turtles and can reach a weight of 1,300 pounds and a length of seven feet. The Kemp's ridley are the smallest, weighing less than 100 pounds. Kemp's ridleys are also the most endangered of the sea turtles. It is estimated that there are only 500 adult females left in the world.

Sea turtles mature slowly. Some, such as the green turtle, may take 30 years or longer to reach maturity. It is not known how long sea turtles live, but it is believed that they can reach a great age if left undisturbed by man.

Most species will migrate long distances from their feeding grounds to their nesting ground. The leatherback nests in the tropics but regularly feeds in cold-water areas such as those around Nova Scotia. The green turtle has been known to navigate thousands of miles to return to a nesting area.

It is widely believed that sea turtles return to the beach where they were hatched to lay their eggs. How they find their way back to nesting areas is still a mystery. Many theories have been proposed, but none has been proven. While sea turtles do not nest every year, when they do, they nest several times in a season.

Female sea turtles lay their eggs on the beach above the high tide line. It is estimated that only one in 1,000 eggs survives to become an adult turtle, and, in fact, many of the newborn turtles are picked off by natural predators, such as crabs, before they ever reach the water. And once they are swept into the sea, sharks, bluefish, mackerel, and other species will make a meal out of the little turtles.

No one knows precisely where the surviving hatchlings go during the first year of their life. Scientist call this the "lost year." In fact, there is much about sea turtles that still remains a mystery. And we may never know, for sea turtles are being driven to the brink of extinction by destruction of their nesting beaches, poaching of their eggs, accidental taking during fishing, and hunting for their meat and shells.

leatherback
laúd

green
verde

flatback
kikila

loggerhead
caguama

hawksbill
carey

Kemp's ridley
golfina

olive ridley
lora

BRATH

Turtles are kept in captivity for over a year so that they may grow larger and become better able to defend themselves when released.

Along the boardwalk are tarot card readers, jugglers, exotic dancers, bead jewelers, sidewalk masseuses, and the Cookie Lady who sells from her bicycle and shouts, "Buy a cookie and we'll both eat tonight." This is where the famous chain saw juggler got his start. He has since moved to the big time in Venice Beach, California, where I had once a chance to catch his act after he graduated from Key West.

One of the tourist attractions in Key West is the Key West Aquarium that maintains a head start program for the endangered green sea turtle. This is an experimental program where hatchlings are

Enjoying a Number 4 at Lands End Marina, Key West.

allowed to grow for a year until they are large enough to survive most of the predators that normally go after the baby turtles, such as crabs and birds. The aquarium also features several grown sea turtles that were brought in by fishermen over the years, including the rare and most endangered Kemp's ridley. It's very difficult to see sea turtles in the wild. We had only caught brief glimpses of four wild sea turtles in all our travels. Many environmental purists complain about any sort of captivity, but I think limited displays are a one good way to raise the public's consciousness to their plight.

Key West is also where I added to my showering repertoire. Earlier, I mentioned the five types of showers available on this cruise. Well, Number 6 came to me after tying up at Lands End Marina and recalling the showering technique of the main character in *The Accidental Tourist* by Anne Tyler. This is where you shower fully clothed and wash your clothes at the same time. *Sabra* was tied to a busy pier at a marina that didn't have shower facilities. It stays light very late in Key West, and I was reluctant to shower naked with the dock hose in full view of the marina, so I left my clothes on and saved myself the problem of doing laundry.

THE MARQUESAS

Michael returned to Washington and Lee, a Florida turtle watcher and marine conservationist, accompanied me to the Marquesas, further west in the Florida Keys. She and I were looking for fresh evidence of green turtle nesting and also evidence of plastic pollution on the beaches and in the mangrove stands on these uninhabited islands.

We were lucky to find turtle crawl tracks made the night before by a large green turtle. We noted that the turtle had made several false crawls onto the beach without digging a nest. The beach was full of plastic debris, beer cans, and bottles. We suspect this foreign matter discouraged the turtle and she headed back to sea to try again the next night. As a matter of fact, the next morning Lee spotted another set of tracks and an accompanying nest. She speculated it was the same turtle by the size and crawl pattern. Had the turtle been turned back once more by the debris, she might have dropped her hundred or so eggs in the sea where they would not have hatched.

While in the Marquesas we met Marshall, a fly casting fishing

Green sea turtle crawl tracks near a nest on the Marquesas Islands.

guide. Marshall specializes in "release fishing" where the catch is
released and allowed to live. The remarkable thing about fly casting
in the Marquesas was seeing anglers go after 40- to 180-pound fighting
tarpon with 15-pound test lines. They fished in the flats where the
water was only three or four feet deep where the fish can easily be seen.
Oftentimes the fisherman had to cast about 100 yards to reach the fish
and then the fish would run off for another 300 yards before finally
being brought in. They fished from skiffs that were silently poled along
these flats. It's quite a sport and the fish indeed deserved to go free for
another time and another fight.

We also met Craig and Devonne at the Marquesas anchorage.

Watching the turtle watcher on the Marquesas.

They were the founders of Reef Relief, a local organization devoted to saving Florida's coral reefs. They were raising funds to pay for mooring buoys at particularly sensitive coral reefs. These buoys would eliminate the damage caused by boats anchoring on the reefs. The motion of anchors and anchor chains can easily devastate 500 years of beautiful coral growth in a matter of minutes.

Craig had just returned from filming a large group of mating sharks in the area. He told me this just after I had spent two hours in the water scraping slime and barnacles off my hull. I guess what you don't know can't hurt you.

Key West and the Marquesas were an experience. On first impressions one wants to stay here forever. It's funky, the weather is sublime, the people are friendly and a little outrageous, and the scenery is beautiful. After a few days you know that your brains are going to turn to mush if you don't hurry north. They told me a story about a luckless soul who had spent too much time in the sun and was last seen living on his 14-foot Sunfish. I got out of there before it was too late.

KEY LARGO
NATIONAL MARINE SANCTUARY

On the way to Palm Beach we stopped at the Key Largo National Marine Sanctuary. We tied up at a mooring provided by the federal government and enjoyed a few hours of snorkeling over the coral reef.

These moorings are an important part of environmental conservation at the sanctuaries. During our brief stay, about a dozen other boats were tied up to moorings and enjoying the reef. Had the moorings not been there, *Sabra* and the other boats would have been anchored on the reef. It is very likely that in the course of a day's visit to the reef these boats with their heavy anchors and anchor chains would have wiped out hundreds of years of beautiful coral growth.

The U.S. has a proud tradition of protection of outstanding natural resources areas. Just over 100 years ago, the natural wonders of Yellowstone were set aside as our first national park. Attempts to conserve part of our nation's marine heritage are at the same stage that our nation's park system was in the late 19th century. Only in 1975 did the U.S. government begin to designate nationally significant marine areas as

DESIGNATED U.S. MARINE SANCTUARIES

THE MONITOR: This first sanctuary, designated in 1975, protects the wreck of the Civil War ironclad *U.S.S. Monitor.* Research at the site off the North Carolina coast has enabled archaeologists to reconstruct a significant period in U.S. history and to insure the preservation of this historic wreck.

KEY LARGO: Located off Key Largo in the Florida Keys and adjacent to John Pennekamp State Underwater Park, this sanctuary protects 100 square nautical miles of spectacular coral reef. Populations of commercially important stone crabs and spiny lobsters and recreational fishing favorites such as grouper, snapper, dolphin fish, and pompano are found in the sanctuary, as are old lighthouses and sunken ships. A mooring buoy system, developed especially for this sanctuary to prevent further anchor damage to the coral reefs, is being used to protect coral reefs in other parts of the Keys, in Hawaii, and in the Caribbean.

CHANNEL ISLANDS: The Channel Islands sanctuary, designated in September, 1980, includes 1252 square miles of water within six nautical miles of the four northern Channel Islands and Santa Barbara Island off southern California. The area is noted for its unusually high biological productivity. Some 30 species of marine mammals are consistently observed here. Kelp beds provide nursery and feeding waters and shelter for many species of fish. Thousands of seabirds, including endangered brown pelicans, rely upon the waters for their sustenance. Sanctuary research, education, and management is fostering a regional approach to conservation of this outstanding but heavily used area.

GULF OF THE FARALLONES: Initially designated in January, 1981 as the Point Reyes/Farallon Islands National Marine Sanctuary, this site covers 948 square miles and is located northwest of San Francisco, California. It is biologically very productive, supporting several species of seals and sea lions and the largest seabird rookeries in the contiguous United States. The protection afforded these waters complements the protection afforded by the adjacent national seashore.

CORDELL BANK: This site is located five miles north of the Gulf of the Farallones marine sanctuary. This submerged mountain supports lush biological communities, including slow-growing, endangered California hydrocoral. Upwelling of nutrients caused by the topography of the bank makes for exceptional productivity which attracts fish, marine mammals, and seabirds.

GRAY'S REEF: This site, also designated in January, 1981, is located off the coast of Georgia. It is perhaps the largest natural "live-bottom" reef along the southeastern coast of the U.S. Limestone outcroppings provide homes for coral and other benthic organisms and shelter and forage areas for fish and sea turtles. Little is known about such live-bottom reefs and marine sanctuary status has contributed to research about their complex ecology and the impacts of human activities on these marine oases.

LOOE KEY: Designated in January, 1981 and covering a five square nautical mile section of the Florida reef tract, Looe Key includes one of Florida's most spectacular coral reefs. The reef's increasing popularity had led to destruction of coral structures through groundings, careless anchoring, and damage by divers. Through education and the establishment of a mooring buoy system, gross damage to the reef has ended. The prohibition of spearfishing in this area has led to the re-appearance of larger fish on the reef.

FAGATELE BAY: This site, located in American Samoa, was designated in April, 1985. Covering 160 acres, this sanctuary contains a coral terrace system that provides a diversity of habitats for marine fishes and sea turtles.

marine sanctuaries. There are now eight marine sanctuaries: Point
Reyes-Farrallon and Cordell Bank, both off Northern California,
Gray's Reef off Georgia, Key Largo off Florida, Channel Islands off
Southern California, Looe Key off Florida, Fagatele Bay off American
Samoa, and the U.S.S. Monitor off North Carolina. *Sabra*'s visit to the
Key Largo sanctuary and our experience with the mooring buoys
reinforced our understanding of the continuing need to wisely manage
the marine environment.

Before departing Palm Beach on the final homeward leg, I was
interviewed by *USA Today* regarding our marine conservation odyssey, and particularly the Cuba trip. We had planned to meet at the
marina so that the reporter could take pictures of *Sabra,* but he warned
me that the interview might be cancelled if he had to attend an
execution scheduled to take place at a Florida prison that morning.
Fortunately, for me and the prisoner, the execution was stayed.

On Being a
Mid-Life Vagabond

†††††
Florida to Chesapeake Bay

T he uneventful six-week journey from Key West to Chesapeake
Bay was the perfect opportunity to review the marine conservation data gathered during *Sabra*'s Caribbean voyage and to
reflect on my personal sailing adventure. The homeward passage also
gave me an opportunity to do some singlehanded offshore sailing,
something I had been reading and dreaming about for the last 10 years.
My major stops on this leg included Charleston, Beaufort, Norfolk,
and finally, Herrington Harbor, just south of Annapolis.

THOUGHTS ON SINGLE-HANDING

The sport of sailing the wide open seas alone is fairly obscure. It
probably ranks right up there with curling and luge racing. Yet, on
the list of most publicized international sailboat races are two single-
handed events—the round-the-world BOC Challenge and the qua-
drennial C-STAR transatlantic race. Some of the most exciting sailing
literature is the work of single-handers: Joshua Slocum, Bernard Moi-
tessier, Dame Naomi James, Phil Weld, Sir Francis Chichester, Tristan

Jones, and Robin Knox-Johnston, to name only a few members of this small and unique breed of loners.

Single-handing up the East Coast was an opportunity to see if I could comfortably handle *Sabra* by myself and if I could live with the emotions of being totally alone in a small boat on such a vast body of water. My personal conclusions on single-handing are mixed.

All told, I only spent about one week single-handing offshore and during most of that time I slept or dozed in the cockpit. I kept an alarm clock close by to wake me every hour or so for a quick scan of the horizon and a glance at the compass. Waking up every half hour is not often enough since a collision with a freighter can occur within 20 minutes of sighting a ship on the horizon. But sleeping for less than 20 minutes at a time would have made me irritable and totally useless. Bumping into a freighter or fishing boat was my biggest worry, but, realistically, the odds of a collision in the open water are pretty small unless you're in busy shipping lanes or fishing grounds. In the shipping lanes freighters are often on autopilot with no one on lookout, as I learned on our return from Cuba, and commercial fishermen have the absolute right-of-way when towing a net.

I found that handling the boat by myself wasn't very difficult and was actually much easier far from shore, where the risks of running into something hard were pretty small. It was much more difficult sailing near shorelines, piers, or in company with other boats in a harbor or channel, than in the relative safety of the open water.

Before leaving the Florida coast for my big single-handing adventure, I had a brief encounter with the U.S. Coast Guard. I was eager to have the best available tide current data for the Fort Pierce inlet that had to be negotiated the next morning. Contrary tidal currents in the narrow inlets along this coast can make boat handling with small auxiliary engines difficult and sometimes dangerous. I decided to check with the Coast Guard station at the inlet for their local knowledge and most up-to-date tidal information.

At the entrance to the station was a big bright sign that asked all persons to "clear their weapons" before entering the building. Upstairs in the visitors office, the on-duty person gave me a copy of the NOAA tide and current tables adding, "I hope you know how to read these tables, because we don't." It was disheartening to learn that the U.S. Coast Guard, the agency responsible for testing ship captains and manning a major inlet, probably knew more about weapons than the daily tidal currents.

On my way out of the station, I decided to photograph the front of the building with the "clear your weapons" sign. As soon as I snapped the picture, an officer ran out and asked what I was doing and whether I had permission to take pictures. I told him that I was simply adding the name of this station to my photo collection of Coast Guard stations. He looked puzzled at my response and for lack of anything better to say, cautioned me to ask for permission the next time I took pictures of a Coast Guard station.

Was it drugs or terrorism that made the officer so nervous about my innocent photography? Ever since the Coast Guard started going after drug traffickers, they seemed to have become more militaristic and less involved in their traditional mission of search and rescue. I appreciate the valuable public service the guard provides, but not being allowed to photograph the front of the station, the enlisted man's inability to read tide tables, and the seemingly pointless weapons sign makes me wonder about their peacetime priorities. The war on drugs is certainly changing the image of the U.S. Coast Guard, and for the worse in my opinion.

I had one amusing incident in the Charleston, South Carolina harbor channel. It was a warm, sunny Sunday afternoon. I had just passed historic Fort Sumter and the gleaming white nuclear freighter, *Savannah*. There were many weekend boaters in the channel and I was feeling particularly pleased with myself for being out there alone and headed out to sea.

Suddenly, and without warning, the mainsail fell down. I couldn't believe my eyes. Here I was feeling competent and relaxed in the cockpit and for no apparent reason over 350 square feet of dacron and five spruce battens decided to stop behaving as a sail and instead crumple into a useless pile on deck. On further inspection, I found that the ties to the yard had frayed from the harsh sunlight and constant boat motion. It was a timely reminder before an offshore passage not to get too self-confident.

Unlike the straightforward routine of single-handed boat handling, emotions are a little harder to deal with and to describe. I didn't enjoy sailing solo as much as I expected I would. I found a need to have someone with whom to share both the good and bad experiences of sailing. At one anxious point along the North Carolina coastline, when I finally spotted the Beaufort Channel light beacon after a difficult piece of nighttime navigation, I shouted out into the dark nothingness, "All right Frankel, you did it." My navigational calcula-

High-level maintenance.

tions were right on the money and I was very proud of my success (with a little help from Mr. Sulu). But it wasn't enough to shout at the waves and blackened sky. I wanted someone to experience and celebrate the accomplishment with me. It was like a graceful slam dunk with nobody in the stands to see it and cheer.

What had made this particular landfall so sweet was that for the first time on this trip I had deliberately sought out the infamous Gulf Stream to take advantage of the northerly current flow. When I calculated my approach and found that *Sabra* had been averaging an amazing eight knots for the past 24 hours, I couldn't believe Mr. Sulu's trusty SatNav report. Then seeing the flashing beacon cut through the

Sabra under sail, Chinese junk-rig style. Photo by Scott Frankel.

darkness right on schedule was an exquisitely rewarding sight.

I also found myself spending far too much time dwelling on catastrophes that might befall *Sabra* and how to deal with them. Most of these events, like being run into by a whale, had a very low probability of occurring—something like the odds of being hit by a rhinoceros on the D.C. Beltway. But the mental exercise of contingency planning crowded out more productive thinking and left me tired, and depressed. It also left me less appreciative of my accomplishments and the beautiful surroundings.

ON BEING A MID-LIFE VAGABOND

I've always wanted to be a vagabond. I wish I had had the opportunity to "do the continent" or some similar adventure before setting out on a professional, career-oriented life. This voyage was to be my belated vagabond adventure. However, I concluded early in the trip that to be a true vagabond you have to cut most if not all of your ties to anything that binds you with a professional life and that includes schedules, telephones, mail, and meetings. Although there were many rewarding, carefree, laid-back, and idyllic moments, I could not escape the need to be productive. Contrary to what my friends and acquaintances might think, I never quite achieved the true vagabond state and that caused me several frustrations.

Telephoning proved to be a particularly annoying and frustrating experience on this trip. I sometimes found myself in a communications office with 30 other people waiting my turn at one of three telephones. When I was lucky enough to find a public telephone with access to an international operator, the operator would sometimes want to verify my credit card number by calling my home before placing the call. I would then try patiently to explain that there was nobody home and the reason I have a credit card was to make calls when I was not at home. This bit of sarcasm would go unnoticed, and I would then feel like I was in the middle of one of Lily Tomlin's famous telephone operator routines. In some countries you need a special plastic card to make calls at pay telephones and these cards are only available at a few locations during working hours. Trying to reach someone at night usually meant rowing ashore after dark to a rickety pier and then wandering around a deserted town looking for a telephone. It was all

"The Tourists," by Chaim Gross in Norfolk, Virginia. *Photo by Image.*

very difficult for someone accustomed to having a telephone at arm's reach and instantly in touch with everyone—or at least their answering machines.

Receiving mail was another minor frustration because I had to identify specific addresses where I could be reached at least two weeks in advance of my arrival. Since I didn't stay anywhere that long and I could never accurately judge my travel time to the next destination, it was difficult to set up a mail schedule. Fortunately, outgoing mail was no problem and I was able to routinely mail off reports and postcards. I gained a new appreciation for the U.S. Postal Service.

Finding the right "office" environment to write reports was another minor, but somewhat amusing problem. I couldn't write much on board *Sabra* because of the boat's motion and the constant interruptions to do some maintenance, check on navigation, trim the sails, or catch up on sleep. It was difficult to lay out all my materials and concentrate on writing for any lengthy period. I was able to do my thinking and organizing on board and save the writing for coffee shops, hotel lobbies, or anyplace that had comfortable seats and a plentiful supply of coffee. One of the best places I ever found for writing was the father's waiting room in the maternity ward of a hospital. It was perfect, close to the marina, air-conditioned, well lit, and stocked with with comfortable seats and foot rests, and lots of free

My morning coffee on Culebra. Photo by Scott Frankel.

"The office" on Antigua. Photo by Scott Frankel.

coffee. Nobody ever came up to ask about my wife or expected child.

Fast-food places also made excellent temporary offices. The tables were clean and there was plenty of coffee at a reasonable price. Also, the waitresses weren't eager to get rid of you because no tips were expected. Hotel lobbies, especially fancy hotels, were my favorite hangouts. As long as I was reasonably well dressed and acted as though I belonged nobody challenged my use of the facilities. I spent many hours at the Omni in Charleston nursing a glass of wine, with a pianist in the background, and plenty of nuts and hors d'oeuvres. The concierge was even nice enough to arrange copying services for my reports.

You just have to know how to use the system. After paying into
the system for many years of business travel, I had learned well.

Another minor frustration concerned arrival and departure
schedules. Everyone at home always wanted to know exactly when I
was scheduled to arrive, where I was going next, and when would I
be departing. On a sailboat, schedules generally require a consultation
with the gods and not with the Official Airline Guide. It was difficult
to make this point with my shore-based compatriots, especially those
who were "scheduled" to meet me somewhere.

Finally, what I missed most in this quasi-professional, quasi-vaga-
bond lifestyle was a word processor. Once you've been introduced to
word processing it's hard to go back to paper and pen. It's like doing
long division without a calculator.

Vagabond life wasn't what I thought it would be and it proved
to be especially difficult in mid-life. Some of my confirmed vagabond
acquaintances tell me that it takes at least a year to get used to the
carefree, no-ties life. But I still can't shake the dream out of my head.
Maybe someday . . .

Concluding
Observations
on the Environment

✝✝✝✝✝✝

S *abra* sailed over 5,000 miles and visited 22 islands in the Caribbean basin to explore and learn more about the marine environment in this region. The six-month journey was an opportunity to see this environment firsthand and to learn about the issues from local officials. The brief time spent in the Caribbean allowed me only an introduction to some of the complex environmental problems facing the islands. However, brief as the voyage was, the impressions reaffirmed the importance of saving the wildlife of these islands and the very sensitive nature of the marine ecosystems around them.

For the most part, the marine environment is as beautiful as the picture postcards and travel brochures of the region. But these views are literally the surface beauty. Beneath these first impressions are the realities of continued exploitation of endangered species, destruction of critical marine habitats, and pollution of the water. *Sabra*'s journey was an opportunity to look behind the postcard scenery and gain a sense of the fragile marine environment and the conservation efforts needed to protect this environment.

WHY THE CARIBBEAN BASIN?

The Center for Marine Conservation has a worldwide interest in the marine environment and the conservation of marine life. It has focused its public policy research and public advocacy efforts on behalf of selected marine species including marine mammals and sea turtles wherever they occur. The Center has also paid particular attention to specific marine habitat issues including the designation of marine sanctuaries. Both of these complementary interests are evident in the Caribbean. Most species of sea turtles inhabit the waters of the Caribbean and the southeastern U.S. The humpback whales of the North Atlantic, that summer off the coast of New England, winter and breed in a newly designated marine sanctuary off the coast of the Dominican Republic. Millions of American tourists vacation in the Caribbean islands, exerting intense environmental stress on the sensitive marine ecosystems. Considerable American investments are used for tourist development in the islands, which in turn increases the pressure of tourism on the environment. The U.S. government has taken steps to increase American investments in the region through the Caribbean Basin Initiative. America has sizeable possessions in the Caribbean and it's quite conceivable that one of these possessions, Puerto Rico, will eventually be our 51st state. These are some of the reasons why the Caribbean basin is important to the Center and why *Sabra* undertook this voyage.

WHAT ARE THE KEY MARINE CONSERVATION ISSUES?

The firsthand observations and local contacts made on this voyage concentrated on six marine conservation issues: widespread plastic pollution in the ocean, conservation of threatened and endangered sea turtles, inauguration and continued management of the newly designated humpback marine sanctuary in the Dominican Republic, increasing destruction of critical mangrove habitat, international trade in endangered species, and the destruction of sensitive coral and sea grasses due to anchoring.

The observations made on each of these issues are summarized below along with recommendations for further activities. These observations are not intended to be an exhaustive analysis of marine problems in the region but rather a starting point from which to identify opportunities for further research, advocacy, and public education programs.

1. The Deceptive Problem of Plastic Debris

During *Sabra*'s 1,000-mile crossing of the Sargasso Sea from the U.S. mainland to the Caribbean, and after many hours of scanning the horizon, I saw very few pieces of plastic debris. This scarcity of plastic, coupled with the crystal clear quality of the water, led me to wonder about the true extent of the plastic pollution problem in the ocean. However, subsequent encounters with large quantities of plastic debris on the most remote island beaches led me to conclude that plastic debris in the ocean is indeed a widespread problem. Its apparent sparseness in the open water hides the true extent of the problem. The vastness of the ocean dilutes the visibility of the plastic, but the beaches counteract this illusion by collecting the plastic debris. It's as though the chain of islands and their beaches are a large sieve catching the debris as the Atlantic currents flow by toward the Gulf of Mexico.

The environmental problems with plastic debris, apart from its unsightliness, are that plastic can resemble food for many species, including endangered sea turtles. Debris entangles marine mammals and seabirds, and, once on the beach, it can interfere with sea turtle nesting. It also presents an economic problem in that discarded plastic fishing nets continue to "fish" valuable resources, foul ship propellers, and mar the beauty of beaches.

Solutions to the plastic debris problem include research into making plastic more degradable, gaining a better understanding of where this debris comes from and who generates it, and the enforcement of laws to curb the dumping of plastics in the ocean. More work is needed on characterizing and monitoring plastic debris in the ocean and passing national and international laws to regulate dumping at sea. The Caribbean offers a unique opportunity to study both the local and international distribution of plastic debris as a result of the ocean currents and the spacing of the islands.

A considerable amount of the plastic debris on the island beaches comes from cruise ships that ply the local waters and from land-generated garbage. A public education program and direct contact with cruise ship operators might help focus attention on plastic dumping by cruise ships, especially since the plastic befouls the very environment they are selling. The nonlocal plastic debris found on the beaches comes from distant fishing operations, commercial shipping throughout the Atlantic, and discarded plastic from the European continent that has drifted across to the islands on the North Atlantic currents. A rigorous examination of the debris washed up on Caribbean beaches could provide important information on its sources and could bolster the need for worldwide plastic dumping regulations and enforcement of the regulations.

2. The Continuing Decline of Threatened and Endangered Sea Turtles

During *Sabra*'s six-month voyage, I saw only four sea turtles in the wild. These sightings occurred in the American and British Virgin Islands. However, I did see several adult and juvenile sea turtles in captivity at the Bitter End Hotel in Virgin Gorda, the Havana aquarium, and a head-start project in a Key West aquarium (where hatchlings are raised until better able to fend for themselves and then released). It's surprising how graceful these reptiles can be and how appealing the very young ones are as they cavort in the tank. I can now see how Glenda Jackson became so attracted to sea turtles in the movie *Turtle Diary*.

There are eight species of sea turtles in the world. Six species are found in the western Atlantic. The southeastern U.S., Gulf of Mexico, and the Caribbean are favorite habitats and nesting grounds for hawksbill, green, Kemp's ridley, olive ridley, leatherback, and loggerhead turtles.

All of these species are threatened or endangered in this region. The decline of sea turtle populations is due to the accidental catching of turtles in fishing operations, the poaching of turtle eggs, the taking of turtles for their meat, the taking of turtles for tortoiseshell, the destruction of nesting beaches due to development and pollution, and the ingestion of or entanglement with plastic debris. All of these activities are evident and continuing in the Caribbean in spite of the fact that sea turtle populations are known to be declining.

Most Caribbean countries have laws to prohibit fishing for turtles during the nesting season and most prohibit the taking of turtle eggs. However, these laws are not well enforced due to a lack of funding and the unpopularity of the laws among the poor fishermen. I was told that interfering with the fishermen's traditional rights to take turtles was very unpopular and almost impossible to enforce.

In Cuba, the government is attempting to increase turtle stocks by head-start and ranching operations rather than by curbing fishermen. Basically this involves keeping hatchlings in captivity until they are large enough to survive some of their natural predators. They then are released to augment the natural stocks of sea turtles. Cuba is also looking forward to farming sea turtles which would be bred and kept in captivity until they were slaughtered for their meat and tortoiseshell. Unfortunately, the success of both such operations, which have been tried elsewhere, is questionable and no proof exists that these techniques improve the wild stocks sufficiently to allow continued fishing for turtles.

Mounting any sort of effort to curb turtle fishing, especially in the underdeveloped Caribbean countries, is probably not very cost-effective. The continuing decline in turtle populations will ultimately ensure that few if any fishermen will go into this business in the future. A more effective approach is through turtle conservation education aimed at children in the school systems. The children will be tomorrow's leaders and in a position to appreciate and protect these species. The Center has a long history and a good reputation in providing public education materials for students and teachers.

Going after local producers of tortoiseshell jewelry would also be a very difficult undertaking in the poor and limited economic climate of these countries. Local producers are simply meeting a demand created by foreign tourists. The tourists are primarily Americans, Canadians, and Western Europeans. It would make more sense to educate these tourists and raise their awareness as to the damage caused by their purchases of endangered species products. This would reduce or eliminate the tortoiseshell market and local artisans would turn to other products to relieve tourists of their dollars and marks. One approach is to display multilingual posters and brochures at various tourist concentration points, such as airports, planes, cruise ships, charter boat centers, and hotels, to warn of the damage caused by purchasing endangered species products.

3. The Humpback Whale Marine Sanctuary
and Other Marine Parks

Sabra had a unique opportunity to sail through the newly designated Silver Bank Humpback Whale Sanctuary off the coast of the Dominican Republic. I was rewarded with several sightings of humpback whales, including one exciting encounter with a 50-foot whale, which came within 10 feet of the boat. This population of endangered humpback whales is the same one that visits the New England coast during the summer months and provides many Americans with unforgettable whale-watching experiences and supports a thriving whale-watching industry.

The president of the Dominican Republic recently declared the Silver Bank area a marine sanctuary. However, the designation is only the beginning. Now Dominicans have a mission to support further research on these endangered whales and an opportunity to manage the area as a true sanctuary for the whales. One of the opportunities open to the Dominicans is the development of a whale-watching industry. This would be a lucrative addition to the growing tourist economy, and, if managed properly, would also add to the research information on the whale population and the public awareness of this endangered species.

The U.S. is in an excellent position to provide Dominicans with guidance for operating a whale-watching business based on years of experience available from similar operations in New England and California. In addition, sanctuary management guidelines, funding for whale researchers, and the printing and distribution of interpretive materials would be effective activities for the Center for Marine Conservation, now that the Silver Bank sanctuary is a reality.

Developing interpretive brochures and poster materials should not be limited to marine sanctuaries. Several of the islands have or are interested in developing national parks which might include marine areas. One of the pressing needs for such parks is the development, printing, and distribution of wildlife materials to go along with the park administration.

4. Development and the Decline of Mangrove Habitat

Mangrove forests form a border between terrestrial and marine ecosystems along tropical coastlines. Like estuaries and wetlands, mangroves provide a rich habitat for many forms of marine life. Mangroves grow throughout the Florida Keys and Caribbean islands. Their location along attractive coastlines brings them into direct conflict with developers. During *Sabra*'s voyage, I saw considerable evidence that mangrove forests had been cleared to expose beaches for tourist hotel development and to provide homesites with a "better" view of the ocean.

The clearing of mangroves is a pervasive and insidious problem in the islands. Unfortunately, there are no specific projects or programs to highlight the consequences of mangrove destruction. The Center has an opportunity to focus attention on the critical role mangroves play in habitat conservation and coastline management. The St. John, U.S. Virgin Islands National Park is an excellent example of an area in need of additional public awareness as well as regulatory measures to control the decline of mangrove forests. Although the actual parkland is protected by the U.S. Park Service, there are many in-park land parcels and adjoining lands that are vulnerable to private development. More work must be done with developers and the general public to draw attention to and protect the mangroves, while at the same time allowing the public access to the coastline. Similar assistance can be provided to other islands contemplating the designation of parks and the control of coastline development.

5. Wildlife Trade in Endangered Species

International trade in wildlife has been responsible for population declines of many endangered marine and terrestrial species. Prime examples of this are found in the trade of tortoiseshell and black coral. At every port visited by *Sabra* where tourists were found I saw tortoiseshell and black coral jewelry for sale. In some instances I also saw stuffed turtle heads and lacquered turtle shells for sale. All eight sea turtle species are protected from the threat posed by international commercial trade by the international treaty known as CITES, the Convention on International Trade in Endangered Species of Wild Fauna and Flora. Ninety-five countries are members of this convention, including the Dominican Republic, Bahamas, and Trinidad and Tobago, and St. Lucia in the Caribbean. Member countries agree to ban, regulate, and monitor trade in endangered or threatened wildlife species.

CITES has established a worldwide system of trade controls for threatened wildlife and wildlife products. Protection is provided for the most endangered species, such as great whales and sea turtles, by member countries agreeing to outlaw trade in such species. For species such as black coral, which might become endangered if trade in them is not controlled and monitored, members require issue permits for their international trade.

The trade that I saw in the Caribbean was either in violation of CITES or in countries that are not members of CITES. There is a continuing need to encourage membership in CITES, to monitor abuses of CITES in member countries, and to provide technical assistance to countries seeking to enhance law enforcement and scientific researches. Specific solutions include encouraging nonmember nations to join CITES, documentation of illegal trade by member countries not enforcing CITES, monitoring trade by nonmember countries to assess the extent of the problem, public awareness and education of tourists who encourage illegal trade through their purchases, and assistance to small countries in setting up the administrative mechanisms by which CITES can be implemented under their laws and jurisdiction.

6. Anchors vs. Coral and Sea Grasses

By design, anchors and anchor chains are made to dig into the bottom. In a contest with the coral and sea grass environment, the environment generally loses. In a matter of minutes, an anchor and its chain can wipe out hundreds of years of slow, steady coral growth. The sharp flukes of an anchor designed to dig in and hold a boat can also dig up sea grasses, roots and all, thus depriving some endangered green sea turtles of their favorite food. The existence of beautiful coral reefs and sea turtle habitats draws boaters to these sensitive areas and their anchors put enormous pressure on these fragile ecosystems.

One solution to this problem is to replace anchoring with regulated moorings. Boaters can be required to tie up to a mooring instead of setting an anchor, as *Sabra* did at moorings provided by the U.S. Park Service in Buck Island off St. Croix and at the Key Largo Marine Sanctuary, as well as similar moorings in the British Virgins. Naturally, the moorings and their maintenance are expensive, but that's not the only reason such moorings are so scarce. The park services are concerned about the potential liability posed if an accident should occur due to a faulty mooring.

The potential benefit of mandatory mooring use should not be restricted to small, private pleasure vessels. Larger moorings could be required for mini-cruise ships that bring tourists closer and closer to sensitive areas for diving and snorkeling. These ships have anchors weighing 2,000 pounds compared to the average 35-pound anchor on a charter sailboat or power boat. The size and weight of these large anchors naturally pose an even greater threat to the environment and make moorings seem even more necessary.

There are at least three other approaches to the anchoring problem. One is the preparation and distribution of brochures to charter yacht centers alerting boaters to the danger posed by anchors, instructing boaters to stay clear of certain identified areas, and describing good anchoring techniques to minimize the damage. This information could also be bound into the many cruising guides to the region. A second approach is to encourage mini-cruise ship operators to consider maintaining their own mooring buoys, or at least avoiding anchoring in well defined, sensitive areas. This approach could be coupled with a study of the liability issue with an aim to limiting such liability for both the government and private mooring operators. Finally, a third approach is to sponsor the private placement of mooring buoys in areas requiring very special protection. These moorings could also carry placards describing the area and its special sensitivity.

ONE MORE ENVIRONMENTAL PROBLEM

On a hot, sultry, windless day on the Chesapeake, *Sabra* quietly nestled into slip E-9 at Herrington Harbor. The mooring lines were made fast, the engine was turned off, and the sails were furled. It was the end of an extraordinary adventure.

Sabra now awaits some TLM, Tender Loving Maintenance, and I am faced with one more environmental dilemma: should I use one of the new, powerful, super-toxic bottom paints on *Sabra*'s hull to prevent barnacles? The paint is deadly to barnacles but it also kills other marine life in the immediate vicinity. The state of Maryland and the federal government have banned the toxic paint effective next year. But in the meantime, do I use it before it becomes illegal and save myself the labor of scraping barnacles next year, or do I do my small part for the marine environment? A difficult choice in an increasingly complex world.

More Reading
on the Caribbean

✝✝✝✝✝✝

The slow, unhurried pace of sailing affords time for contemplative leisure reading. I made use of the opportunity to bone up on the Caribbean, its culture, history, and marine life. Here's a short and eclectic list of references to the Caribbean that I found useful in my travels:

Fidel: A Biography of Fidel Castro, by Peter G. Bourne
   A former White House official in the Carter administration traces the history of Fidel Castro and the emergence of Cuba from an economic appendage to the U.S. to a struggling socialist country.

A Nation of Oceans by Michael Weber and Richard Tinney
   The authors describe the various marine ecosystems to be found in the United States's 88,000 miles of tidal shoreline and over 2.2 million square miles of ocean under our direct economic control.

From Columbus to Castro by Eric Williams
   The history of the Caribbean is dominated by the history of sugar, which is inseparable from the history of slavery, which was inseparable,

until recently, from the systematic degradation of labor in the region. The author presents an authoritative account of this neglected and misrepresented area of the world. Eric Williams was the prime minister of Trinidad and Tobago from the country's independence in 1962 until his death in 1981.

Don't Stop the Carnival by Herman Wouk

This novel is an amusing tale of a high-powered New York press agent who attempts to slow down and enjoy the good life by buying a resort hotel on a mythical Caribbean island.

Easy in the Islands by Bob Shacochis

This collection of short stories reveals the culture and bittersweet life of the Caribbean paradise.

So Excellent a Fishe by Archie Carr

An authoritative account of sea turtles by a world expert in the field. Archie Carr was the director, until his death, of the turtle research center at Tortuguero, Costa Rica, the last major green turtle rookery in the Caribbean. He provides a fascinating and very readable account of one of the most spectacular navigators in the animal kingdom.

The Log of Christopher Columbus translated by Robert Fuson

Columbus resolved to ". . . write everything that I might do and see and experience on this voyage, from day to day and very carefully." The original logs presented to Queen Isabela were lost. Fortunately, two hand transcriptions had been commissioned and the author combines these in an authoritative and scholarly translation of the original logs. This translation also reflects the new landfall theory promoted by the National Geographic.

Cruising Guide to the Caribbean and Bahamas by J. Hart and W. Stone

An island by island, port by port, and anchorage by anchorage description of this region. The authors have provided a detailed physical description along with some cultural insights to aid the cruising sailor.

The Sargasso Sea by John and Mildred Teal

The authors document the accounts of an oceanographic research voyage through the Sargasso Sea. Included in the narrative are detailed descriptions of the physical oceanographic features as well as the varied life forms found in this desert sea.

THE CENTER FOR
MARINE CONSERVATION

The Center for Marine Conservation, with a membership of over 100,000, is the nation's leading organization dedicated to conservation of the marine environment. Their work focuses on four major goals:

- **Conserving marine habitats**

- **Preventing marine pollution**

- **Managing fisheries for conservation**

- **Protecting endangered marine species**

To further these goals, the Center conducts policy-oriented research, promotes public education and citizen involvement, and supports domestic and international laws and programs for marine conservation. The Center has always sought to improve the protection and conservation of marine wildlife and their habitats, through responsible advocacy rather than through confrontation. The Center's view is that permanent changes can best be achieved through cooperation and understanding.

Appendixes

✝✝✝✝✝

Back to the Future

✝✝✝✝✝

The Modern Chinese Junk Rig

When one has
Good wine,
A graceful junk
And a maiden's love,
Why envy the immortal Gods?

LI PO

In his wonderfully illustrated book *Ships of China,* Valentin Sokoloff writes that "a handcrafted sailing ship is a living thing with its own character and charm. A Chinese junk is even more so, and no wonder, as it was invented by an offspring of a nymph and a rainbow. His name was Fu Hsi, the first great ruler who, they say, was born in 2852 B.C. Then Lu Pan, founder of the art of carpentry, greatly improved the original design. Further generations of Chinese shipwrights gave Chinese junks their final seaworthy and practical shape."

The evolution of sailboat design in the West has taken place over a much shorter period of time and on a much different tack. Today the epitome of Western design is represented by America's Cup contenders and high-tech boats designed to compete in such ocean races as in the single-handed transatlantic C-STAR, the BOC Around-the-world Challenge and the Whitbread round-the-world race. Shades of these Bermuda-rigged competitors are seen in virtually every contemporary racing and cruising boat to come off the showroom floor. For the most part, the emphasis in these designs is on speed, particularly performance to windward. There are obviously other aspects to sailing, especially to cruising. And that is where the Chinese junk-rigged boat comes in.

Several crusading Western sailors and boat designers including Thomas Colvin, Angus Primrose, Blondie Hasler, Jock McLeod, and Alan Boswell have long seen the distinct advantages of the Chinese lug rig as being far superior to the conventional rig, especially for short-handed sailing and comfortable cruising. They succeeded in marrying the basic junk design features to modern materials, replacing bamboo and grass mats with aluminum alloy and Dacron. The resulting modern junk rig is designed for the family crew, single-hander, or shorthanded cruising sailors. The junk rig can be easily handled without requiring strength or endurance, and without leaving the safety of the cockpit. Sailing with this rig can be relaxed, enjoyable and safe. It is a rig that is easily reefed, efficient for self-steering, and can do anything that modern rigs can do with much less strain on the crew or the boat. Foremost, it is a rig for a seamanlike passage; safe, quick, comfortable, and able to handle any sailing emergency likely to be encountered.

ELEMENTS OF THE JUNK SAIL

At first sight the rig's unusual appearance, as shown by the typical sail plan, may be confusing to the western eye, but in effect it is extraordinarily simple, clever, and extremely easy to handle. The lug sails have full-length battens which lie across the width of the sails, from luff to leech, and divide the sails into panels. The top batten is the yard, which is a heavier spar than the other battens and takes the full weight of the sail. The bottom batten is the boom, which takes very little load and therefore need be no stronger than the other battens.

The head of the sail is secured to the yard, and the sail is raised from the cockpit by hauling on the halyard, which includes a purchase system between the yard and masthead. The sail is held to the mast by batten parrels that run loosely around the mast at each batten. The luff of the sail always lies on the same side of the mast and extends forward of the mast, making it a balanced lug sail. On one tack the sail lies against the mast and is held off the mast by the battens. On the other tack, the sail hangs away from the mast and is held by the rope parrels.

A multiple topping lift system known as lazyjacks passes under the boom and lies on both sides of the sail forming a cradle, which holds the sail when it is reefed or furled. Two additional parrel lines are led

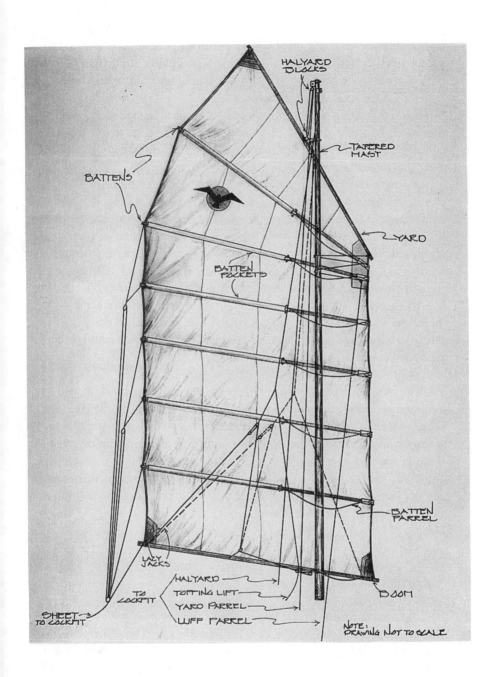

HALYARD
BLOCKS

BATTENS

TAPERED
MAST

YARD

BATTEN
POCKETS

BATTEN
PARREL

LAZY
JACKS

SHEET
TO COCKPIT

TO
COCKPIT

HALYARD
TOPPING LIFT
YARD PARREL
LUFF PARREL

BOOM

NOTE:
DRAWING NOT TO SCALE

back to the cockpit to control the fore-and-aft position of the sail. The yard parrel is used to bring the yard snugly against the mast. This is only important when the sail is reefed and the sail would have a tendency to swing aft of the mast.

Similarly, a luff parrel line is used to prevent the sail from swinging too far forward of the mast and to maintain tension on the luff of the sail. Both of these lines are used to shift the position of the sail and fine-tune the rig.

A single sheet system controls the after end of the boom and the five lower battens by a system of spans (sheetlets) and blocks. This gives control over the entire leech of the sail, not just the boom, and reduces the twist of the sail. The main part of the sheet system is one long length of line that runs through blocks and forms a purchase system so that loading on the tail end is light. The portion of the balanced lug sail forward of the mast performs an important function contributing to the safety and comfort of this rig. When the wind and boat direction conspire to create an accidental jibe, the small portion of the sail in front of the mast actually dampens the motion of the sail and therefore slows down an otherwise violent motion. Both intentional and accidental jibing become much less hair-raising.

The lug rig mast is stepped through the deck to the keel and is designed to stand unsupported. The loads are exerted at the partners where the mast passes through the deck and at the heel of the mast where it is stepped on the keel. The hull and deck are reinforced in these areas. However, the load on the hull is less than that imposed by conventional rigs, where taut shrouds and the highly tensioned forestay and backstay combine to produce tremendous compression loading on the mast and stresses on the hull.

EASY REEFING

The combination of battens, parrels, and topping lifts makes the lug sail the fastest and easiest of all to handle and reef. To reef a lug sail, the halyard is eased from the safety of the cockpit and the sail comes down rapidly under its own weight between the lazyjacks, which collect the sail and hold it on top of the boom. The battens prevent the sail from billowing out, and their own weight plus the sheet system keeps them down. This makes it unnecessary to tie any

reef points or to handle the sail in any way. As soon as the halyard
is eased and sail starts to drop, the sheets slacken, the sail starts to spill
the wind, and the boat begins to weathercock. Unlike other sails, the
lug sail will not flog and damage itself. Being able to raise and lower
sails in increments like Venetian blinds provides an infinite combination of sail plans to balance the rig. The ability to vary sail area with

a variety of fore and aft sail combinations is especially helpful to the boat's tracking ability and the efficient use of wind vane steering.

PERFORMANCE

How does the lug rig perform? It loses some efficiency to windward but regains it in effortless tacking maneuvers and in superior running and reaching. Off the wind, the battens spread the sails to exploit the maximum surface area. This is especially important in light air, when conventional sails have a tendency to collapse. However, apart from speed, the rig provides exceptional performance characteristics, including:

More comfortable and upright ride because the round sectioned, free-standing mast is designed to be flexible so that it bends rather than the boat heeling. The mast acts as a giant shock absorber for the sudden forces of wind and sea. Sailing becomes less tiring and more enjoyable.

Less hazardous sailing for the shorthanded sailor or the family crew, because all sail handling can be done from the safety and the comfort of the cockpit. There is no acrobatic deck work and tacking is just a matter of ignoring the sheets and putting the tiller over.

More stowage space below deck because the sails are permanently rigged and there is no need for extra sails.

Peace and quiet for the experienced sailor and the novice because the fully battened sails do not flog noisily and the control lines do not slap the deck like the Bermudan jib sheets when tacking.

Less wear and tear because of less tension in the control lines, sails, and spars. Chafe and wear on lines and blocks is minimal and gear lasts longer.

Simple construction and maintenance is made possible with flat-cut sails, simple but reliable knots and splices in the rigging, and common materials and engineering. Repairs are simple and materials are readily and cheaply available anywhere in the world.

Big safety factor is built in because the failure of a single pin or shackle cannot bring down the mast. There is no highly stressed standing rigging. Heavy weather sailing is safer, more comfortable, and less of a strain on the hull and crew.

Many sails in one are possible because the Chinese junk rig can match every combination of foresail and mainsail with an infinite variety of settings. Compared to the Bermuda rig, it is slightly less efficient to windward, but off the wind the fully battened sails are more efficient because they present more effective sail area and have no tendency to collapse in light air.

A bonus when aground or in a man overboard situation is gained because the sails drop in seconds, by gravity alone, when the halyards are released. This can all be accomplished from the safety of the cockpit and the sails are automatically stowed with the booms in the topping lift systems.

Less damage from accidental jibes is possible because the balanced lug sail dampens the otherwise violent swings of the sail and boom during a controlled or accidental jibe.

Off-wind efficiency is gained because full-length battens spread the sails for maximum effective sail area. Together with ease of tacking, the increased off-wind efficiency compensates for any loss in windward performance.

The key features of the Chinese junk rig are ease of handling, simplicity to use, and self-furling for the shorthanded crew. These features may not contribute to an America's Cup contender but they do add up to safe, relaxed, and efficient cruising with an emphasis on comfortable and safe passagemaking. The junk rig may not be the answer for everyone, but it is an interesting alternative to the conventional Bermudan cruiser.

The Gulf Stream Lady

✝✝✝✝✝

Many boaters along the east coast of the United States have had
memorable experiences with the Gulf Stream. This immense oceanographic feature of the North Atlantic Ocean, only a few miles off the
coasts of Florida, the Carolinas, and Georgia, extends all the way across
the Atlantic to Norway. It is a force to be reckoned with for anyone
contemplating a passage to Bermuda, the Caribbean, the Bahamas or
an Atlantic crossing.

In contrast to the awesome dimensions and intimidating force of
the Gulf Stream is the ebullient and unassuming government spokesperson for the whereabouts of this major ocean current. Jenifer Clark
is "The Gulf Stream Lady." She is an oceanographer at the National
Oceanographic and Atmospheric Administration, NOAA, who gives
new meaning to the phrase "I'm from the government and I'm here
to help you." Jenifer is a big help to thousands of fishermen and
hundreds of ocean racers who closely monitor the exact location of the
Gulf Stream to help locate fish and to win races.

Five days a week, Jenifer prepares a hand-drawn chart, based on
satellite data, showing the Gulf Stream location as it meanders across
the Atlantic and spawns warm and cold water eddies along its trail.
The applications of the chart include providing information on the

air/sea interface dynamics to the National Weather Service for its weather forecasts; search and rescue information for the Coast Guard; shipping information; and fishing and sailing information. Fishermen read the temperature differences in these charts as a clue to the whereabouts of fish. Sailboat racers find the location of meanders and eddies essential in plotting favorable courses that take advantage of the current, sometimes as much as five knots, and avoiding unfavorable passages that can stop a sailboat dead in its tracks.

Every year, Jenifer is invited to New England for Bermuda Race briefings where she advises racers on the latest satellite determined position of the Gulf Stream. To this she adds her considerable experience in estimating the location of meanders and eddies during the course of the race. Jenifer is often joined by her husband Dane Clark, a meteorologist with NOAA. Between the two of them they make a very helpful contribution to prerace planning. Once underway, racers can receive Jenifer's daily charts via weather facsimile (fax) equipment to keep up-to-date on the movement of the stream's meanders and the all important eddies.

HOW THE EDDIES ARE FORMED

As the Gulf Stream moves eastward off the Cape Hatteras toward Europe it often turns sharply north or south for a brief period forming loops called meanders. The continental shelf and slope waters north of the stream are colder than the Sargasso Sea waters south of the stream. As the meanders encircle these waters and get pinched off and bypassed by the main current, eddies are formed. A northward, clockwise encirclement of warmer Sargasso Sea waters becomes a warm water eddy. Similarly, a southward, counterclockwise encirclement of colder slope waters becomes a cold water eddy. As the eddies become isolated from the Stream they drift westward or southwestward at about two kilometers per day keeping their rotating currents for months or even years. The cold water eddies are generally faster and can attain currents of up to six knots, thereby creating a strong incentive either to avoid the eddy or take advantage of it by being on the correct side.

Jenifer started monitoring the Gulf Stream in 1976, a little more than 200 years after Benjamin Franklin first charted the Gulf Stream to help speed mail delivery to and from England. Although she has moved organizationally within the government agency at least four times, she has managed to keep the Gulf Stream monitoring project as her baby. Her dedication to this project shows in her enthusiasm and willingness to explain everything about this mysterious current.

If it's a clear day when she gets up, she eagerly sets off for work knowing that there is a good chance she'll receive a clear photo from the two 800-plus-kilometer high, polar orbiting satellites. The remote sensors on these satellites have a one-kilometer resolution and produce some outstanding photographs (see accompanying photograph with Cape Cod in the upper left and Bermuda in the lower right). The two satellites produce two pictures per day of this region compared to the geostationary satellite which produces a photograph every 30 minutes from an altitude of 42,550 kilometers. However, the geostationary satellite photograph has a resolution of only eight kilometers.

In over eight years on the job, Jenifer has amassed a prodigious amount of statistics on the Gulf Stream. Most of these statistics are based on the remote temperature measurements by the satellites. The Gulf Stream is considerably warmer than the surrounding Atlantic waters. Therefore, the location of the stream and the eddies that break off of its meanders can be seen as differing shades of grey in the infrared image. The darker grey areas in the photograph represent warmer waters and light gray denotes cooler water. The white areas are clouds.

Jenifer prepares hand-drawn temperature charts, including the location of the Gulf Stream and the eddies, from this type of photographic image. Every week, on Monday, Wednesday, and Friday she issues the portion of the chart north of Hatteras. On Tuesday and Thursday, she issues the southern portion including the Gulf of Mexico and Northern Caribbean.

With all this data it is also possible to show the statistical limits of the Gulf Stream over time. The accompanying chart shows the area over which the stream has wandered over a five-year period from 1980 to 1985. For example, if you don't have an up-to-the-minute location chart and you want the best chance of avoiding the northbound current on your way south along the Florida coastline, stay west of the 80th meridian. In the five-year period depicted on this chart, the main part of the stream has never strayed west of this longitude.

If you want to participate in over 200 years of Gulf Stream data collection efforts, you can volunteer some important information from your own encounters with the Gulf Stream. Government researchers are always in need of actual water temperature data in and around the

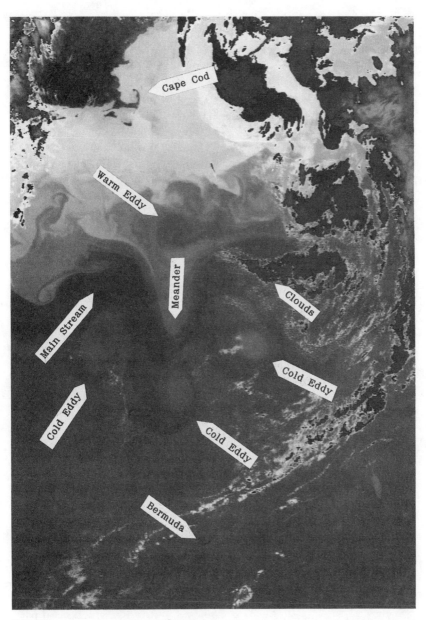

Satellite photo courtesy of NOAA.

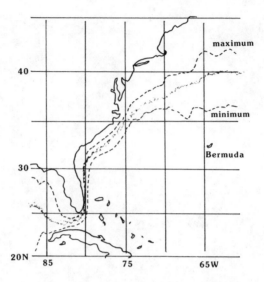

Gulf Stream to use as "surface truth" comparisons with the remote satellite data. Simply take frequent temperature measurements along your track and relate these to your Loran or SatNav position fixes. Use the fixes to estimate the current speed and direction. Send this data to Jenifer Clark, NOAA, Ocean Products Center, Washington, D.C. 20233. Include your position log with the temperature and current data so that information can be plotted accurately alongside the satellite data. Your data, along with data from unmanned buoys, research vessels, and commercial ships, go into making the Gulf Stream one of the best monitored ocean currents on this globe. And no piece of this watery planet has a more helpful and cheerful spokesperson than Jenifer Clark.

The Sargasso Sea

✝ ✝ ✝ ✝ ✝

Most sailors would be hard put to locate the Sargasso Sea on a chart. Yet, whenever they venture southward or eastward a couple of days' sail from the eastern seaboard and beyond the Gulf Stream, they are entering the mysterious Sargasso Sea. A trip from Newport, Rhode Island to Bermuda, an Atlantic crossing, or a passage from North Carolina to the Caribbean will take them through one of the most fabled, remarkable, and least understood seas of the world.

The Phoenicians may have discovered the Sargasso Sea five centuries B.C., as evidence of artifacts washed up on the Azores at the eastern limit of the Sargasso indicates. They may have contributed to the frightening tales of this region in order to keep their trade routes a secret. Ponce de Leon first described the Gulf Stream, which forms the western border to the Sargasso, on his visit to Florida in 1513. But Columbus is credited with the first documented description of this sea as he encountered the mysterious sargassum weed. It wasn't until later that this weed got its name from Portugese fishermen who likened the weed to grapes—*salgazo*—because of the grapelike gas bladders that keep sargassum afloat.

WHERE EXACTLY IS THE SARGASSO SEA?

The exact location of the Sea has been one of the great mysteries surrounding this unique body of water. At first its borders were defined by the currents that "cage" the North Atlantic gyre. A gyre is a huge revolution of surface water driven by winds, salinity and temperature differences, and the rotation of the earth, which imparts a twist known as Coriolis force. Later, the borders of the Sargasso were defined by the presence of sargassum weed. Surveys of this floating weed were recorded and then a line was drawn around the outer occurrences of the weed. Still later it was observed that the Sargasso is both considerably warmer and saltier than the surrounding Atlantic. The saltiness of the Sargasso stems from its isolation from melting polar ice or the inflow of freshwater streams. It is so salty that it can easily be distinguished from the surrounding waters by taste.

Based on the warmer and saltier characteristics, the ever shifting Sargasso Sea can be located between the 20th and 40th north parallels

and the 30th and 70th west meridians, or roughly between the Chesa-
peake-Gibraltar and Puerto Rico-Dakar latitudes and the longitudes of
the Azores and Bahamas. The horse latitudes in the calms between the
easterlies and westerlies, where the Spanish are said to have dumped
horses that dies of thirst, run right through the Sargasso Sea. The
Sargasso Sea is the only named sea without land borders. It is completely surrounded by the Atlantic Ocean.

Another fascinating aspect of the Sargasso's borders is that it has
no sea floor. It is like an oil drop floating on water. Its lens-shaped
warmer and saltier water rides above the colder Atlantic waters. In fact,
it is about two feet higher in the middle than the surrounding Atlantic
due to the pileup of water caused by the Coriolis force. In profile, it
looks like half a peach pit with a deep center and sharp, tapered edges.
Most noticeable to the eye is the intense blue clarity of the water. The
water is remarkably transparent due to the lack of microscopic plant
and animal life and the lack of sediments normally associated with near
shore waters that are fed by nutrient rich land runoff. The blueness
stems from the reflection of the sky unimpeded by foreign matter
which normally absorbs different spectra of light rays.

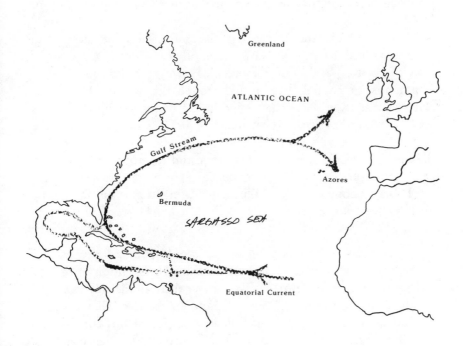

LIFE IN THE DESERT SEA

Probably the most enigmatic quality of the Sargasso Sea comes from the occurrence of sargassum. This weed is part of the algae family and forms the only habitat in an otherwise "desert" sea. Early tales told of ships snared by huge floating beds of sargassum slowly revolving in the Atlantic gyre until they were trapped in the calm, windless center of the sea. The sargassum was also supposed to hide monsters and giant serpents. Even though Columbus disproved these imaginative fables, the mystery persists. One reason for this is that scientists aren't absolutely sure about the origins of sargassum. The weed seems to have come from coastal beds that were torn away during storms. But then they evolved into an ocean plant capable of reproducing nonsexually, vegetatively, and indefinitely without any roots or holdfasts. In the quiet, undisturbed waters at the center of the sea, scientists believe that individual sargassum weeds may be centuries old and the plants visible today may have been alive during Columbus' voyage in 1492!

Animal life in the Sargasso is also shrouded in mystery. The sargassum weed is the only "oasis" in an otherwise desert sea with the lowest plankton level of all the oceans. However, a dense and varied community of animals live in and around this weed habitat. It is believed that baby sea turtles reside in the weeds during their "lost year." Scientist have tracked hatchlings on beaches and juveniles in the open ocean. But they aren't sure where their first year is spent when the animal is small, in need of small foodstuff to grow, and easy prey to a host of predators. The Sargasso Sea may be the answer.

Eels are another mystery. Elisabeth Mann Borgese, in *The Drama of the Oceans,* writes:

> The eels of the Atlantic—so it would appear—have an international organization, with an annual convention in the Sargasso Sea near Bermuda. They arrive there all the way from the rivers of Europe as well as from the Americas. They dive and spawn there, in the thick floating weeds of this current-bound ocean within an ocean—itself a mystery to science and

fraught with lore and legend, a terrible trap where plant filaments and seaweed grip vessels in an unbreakable net. Then the young larvae depart, and though they all seem alike, those of European parentage take up the long journey, riding the Gulf Stream and the North Atlantic Current for three years to the coast of Europe. The American members of this puzzling organization have it easier. It takes them only six months along the Gulf Stream to make their way into the American rivers from which their parents came. The larvae have grown into elvers by the time they reach their destined rivers, in which they take up their freshwater life, to be washed back again into the ocean. After 10 years they embark on the long, hazardous return voyage to the faraway Sargasso Sea. What signal starts them, what compass guides them, no one knows.

IS THERE A DEVIL'S TRIANGLE?

No ancient fables about the Sargasso Sea can match the modern-day chilling mystery surrounding the Devil's Triangle. Also known as the Bermuda Triangle, this piece of the Sargasso extends from Miami to Bermuda to Puerto Rico and back to Miami. Since the end of World War II, a series of strange and unexplained disasters have befallen planes and ships in this region. Officials and scientists have no clues to the disappearances of a fleet of military planes, a 350-foot

freighter, a four-engine commercial plane, and countless smaller craft. UFOs, time space warps, and gargantuan currents that suck vessels into "the abyss" have been blamed for the disappearances, but this western edge of the Sargasso remains a legend yet to be explained by modern science.

PLASTIC POLLUTION

One of the not so mysterious characteristics of the Sargasso Sea is its ability to trap plastic debris. The slow moving currents that encircle the sea and contain the long-lived sargassum also entrap the millions of tons of persistent plastic products dumped annually into the sea by passing cruise ships, fishermen, commercial vessels, recreational boaters, and land-based runoff that eventually makes it to the ocean. Styrofoam cups, six-pack ring holders, plastic jugs, garbage bags, tampon applicators, and discarded fishing nets, are all part of this modern "weed" floating endlessly in the ocean. The plastic lives forever, and that which escapes the Atlantic gyre ends up on swimming beaches, wildlife beaches, and as a visual assault to beautiful coastlines and island beaches.

In addition to acid rain, pesticide runoff, and tar balls, the plastics may destroy the mysteries of the Sargasso long before we have a chance to unravel the legends and scientific curiosities surrounding this remarkable and fragile ocean desert.

Countless boat voyagers will continue to traverse the southwestern portion of the North Atlantic, noting the clarity of the warm water and the floating sargassum weed, without ever realizing that they are in the midst of the mysterious Sargasso Sea.

Plastic Debris and Entanglement

✝✝✝✝✝

More Than a Litter Problem

Since its invention more than 40 years ago, plastic has become such an integral part of life that it is difficult to survey one's surroundings without finding plastic items in use: packaging and containers, household goods, furnishings, equipment and machines. But what happens to plastic that falls into disuse? Unfortunately, the durable characteristics that have made plastic so convenient for packaging, household products, and commercial equipment also make it a continuing, nonbiodegradable, and persistent presence in the environment. A growing body of evidence indicates that when discharged, lost or abandoned in the marine environment, plastic debris adversely affects the oceans and their inhabitants in a multitude of ways.

Environmental impact arises from entanglement of marine animals in plastic debris and from ingestion of plastics by marine organisms. Plastic debris can cause potential threats to humans when divers become entangled or vessels become fouled in debris. The depletion of fishery resources, vessel damage, and aesthetic degradation resulting in lost tourism revenues or costly cleanup procedures all contribute to significant economic impact.

Even though marine pollution has been an issue since the '70s, the issue of plastic debris in the marine environment is a relatively new concern, and sources of hard data are meager. No central data collection source exists to document what types of plastic are out there, where it comes from, what it does, or who is responsible for it. What legal authorities do exist to address ocean pollution have not been used to focus on the particular problem of entanglement of marine animals in plastic debris. Only one federal program exists that targets the problem directly. While federal wildlife managers and those engaged in management of our nation's refuges and seashores are aware of the magnitude of the problem posed by plastic debris, conservation agencies in coastal states seem unfamiliar with the issue, and are generally doing little or nothing to combat the tons of plastic litter that line their beaches. In a recently released federal plan defining priorities for ocean research for the next five years, plastic debris and associated entanglement and ingestion by marine animals ranked among the last four items of a 50-issue list, categorized only as "low priority" national issues.

ENVIRONMENTAL IMPACTS

Frequent reports of the mortality of marine mammals, sea turtles, seabirds, and fish attributed to plastic debris have concerned scientists, conservationists, fishermen, and others in recent years. Plastic in the marine environment may be a problem not only for individual animals, but may ultimately affect entire marine ecosystems.

While plastic debris has been shown to affect individual species, very little is known about the broader impacts on marine populations, communities or ecosystems. To date, extensive research has only been carried out on northern fur seal populations. But among those species that appear to have the greatest degree of interaction with marine plastic debris, many are endangered or threatened species. These include the Hawaiian monk seal, brown pelican, Kemp's ridley, hawksbill, leatherback, green, and olive ridley sea turtles. The effects of plastic debris on these endangered and threatened species therefore should be closely monitored.

Among the species of marine mammals reported entangled, seals and sea lions appear to most vulnerable, which is attributed to their tendency to investigate floating debris. The most common items found on entangled pinnipeds are fragments of nets, and plastic strapping bands used to bind packages. For many pinnipeds, the effects of entanglement on species survival are generally unknown. But for the northern fur seals of the Pribilof Islands in Alaska, recent studies indicate that this population is declining at an annual rate of four to eight percent per year, largely due to entanglement. Assorted types of fishing gear are the most common plastic items found on entangled sea turtles, whereas birds become entangled primarily in monofilament fishing line and six-pack connectors used to carry beverage cans.

Another major problem tied to plastic debris is the issue of ghost fishing, or the ability of lost or discarded fishing gear to continue to catch finfish and shellfish indefinitely. Free-floating gill nets have been reported to trap large numbers of commercially valuable species of finfish and shellfish years after they have been lost. Quantitative estimates of this type of plastic debris from New England's Atlantic gill net fisheries range from 30 miles of lost nets in 1985 to more than 18 miles lost in 1986. Lost trawl webbing turned up on Alaskan beaches in 1974 in quantities of 272 kilograms per kilometer of beach, an amount that dropped to 172 kilograms 10 years later, but only after a significant decrease in the area's trawl fishery. In various fisheries that utilize traps constructed either partially or entirely of plastic, ghost fishing also poses a serious threat to fishery stocks. In New England, it is estimated that 20 percent of 2.5 million lobster pots are lost annually. Off Florida in the Gulf of Mexico, 25 percent of 96,000 stone crab traps were lost in 1984. It is estimated that more than 30,000 crab traps have been lost in Alaskan waters since 1960, 10 percent per year of those set. Each of these pots and traps continues to capture fish and shellfish, resulting in a continuing cycle of baiting and capturing valuable commercial species that are never retrieved.

Along with the increasing reports of plastic debris in the marine environment there has been an increase in the documentation of plastic ingestion by marine animals. Certain animals may ingest plastics nonselectively while feeding on other organisms, while others mistake floating plastic for authentic food items. The ingestion of plastic bags and sheeting by sea turtles has become widely documented and is attributed to deliberate consumption by turtles who mistake these items for jellyfish. To date, 50 species of seabirds have also been known to ingest plastic debris, most commonly polyethylene pellets, which are the raw form of plastic after it has been synthesized from petrochemicals.

ECONOMICS AND SAFETY

In addition to the ecological impacts caused by plastic debris, there are also economic problems. Probably one of the most costly impacts to fishermen is the loss of synthetic fishing gear. Since U.S. fishermen are not required to report fishing gear losses there is no way to assess this. Ghost fishing by lost fishing gear could be severely depleting fishery stocks, but quantitative data on this problem is also limited.

Plastic debris has also been reported to interfere with vessel operations, the most common instances involving plastic items that foul propellers and clog cooling water intake systems. The types of plastic debris involved in these incidents range from entire gill nets to garbage bags, sheeting, and monofilament fishing line. Although this appears to be a problem nationwide, there is no source of documentation to determine the frequency of this occurrence. The fact that some boating supply companies have built devices for propellers to combat this problem, however, may give some indication that it is not merely a random occurrence.

Plastic debris may also pose a threat to human safety in the marine environment. Occasionally divers have become entangled in monofilament fishing line, but more frequently encounters involve gill nets. The disablement of vessels caused by plastic debris may also endanger human safety when power or steering control is lost; some have attributed fatalities at sea to vessel disablement during storms, whereas disabled vessels near inshore structures face the risk of collision. Research and military submarines have had similar near fatal encounters with lost gill nets.

Many coastal communities incur the costs of routine cleanup of debris, while others employ enforcement officers to patrol and control litter deposited by beach goers. In certain areas, regular deposits of large amounts of debris are coming from distant land-based or offshore sources. At Padre Island National Seashore in Texas, 90 percent of beach debris comes from the Gulf of Mexico and consists largely of plastic items associated with merchant shipping and oil industry activities, such as large pieces of plastic sheeting and domestic wastes in quantities and container sizes suggestive of commercial activities. While this problem is costly in terms of cleanup, it may have an even greater impact on the coastal tourist industry. The economic impact suffered by coastal businesses as a result of marine debris was clearly demonstrated by the "floating episode" of June 1988, when unusually large amounts of materials, primarily plastics, washed up on beaches in Long Island. The total cost of the cleanup was one hundred thousand dollars, but an even greater economic loss was suffered by the coastal recreational industry due to the aesthetic degradation of beach areas.

SOURCES OF PLASTIC DEBRIS

Although plastic debris may be generated both on land and at sea, it is generally believed that most of the debris in the marine environment comes from ocean sources. The amount of debris generated worldwide by ocean sources in the early 1970s was estimated to be about 6.4 million metric tons per year. While accidental loss of plastic items from ocean sources contributes to the problem of debris, deliberate disposal at sea is a greater problem. Deliberate disposal of such enormous quantities of waste may be explained in part by several factors. For example, alternative means of handling shipboard wastes such as grinders, compactors and incinerators are not only costly, but under certain circumstances highly undesirable. Furthermore, vessels that store garbage on board require adequate facilities on shore for disposal, but many ports both in the United States and abroad are ill-equipped for handling these wastes.

Commercial fishing operations are a major source of wastes and plastic gear in the ocean. Fishing gear may become lost accidentally due to gear failure caused by normal wear and tear, operational mistakes, and storms. Gear collisions in areas where both fixed and towed gear are used may also contribute to the accidental and, in some instances, deliberate loss of fishing gear. During gear mending procedures, pieces of fishing gear are discarded, whereas entire nets, in particular gill nets, may be deliberately discarded when the total catch is too great to be hauled in. There are also reports of foreign fishermen cutting loose their nets when the U.S. Coast Guard has spotted them fishing in an illegal manner or location. However, extensive documentation of such deliberate gear losses is lacking.

In 1984, there were 24,000 commercial fishing vessels over five gross tons registered in the United States. According to the most recent (1977) regional breakdown, more than half operate in the North Pacific and a large portion of the remaining vessels operate in the Gulf of Mexico. Not surprisingly, the greatest amount of plastic debris generated by this source has been found in the North Pacific.

The worldwide rate of disposal of domestic litter from merchant ships has been estimated at 110,000 metric tons, less than one percent of which is plastic. The amount of cargo-associated wastes including dunnage, shoring, pallets, wires, and covers, is estimated at 5.6 million metric tons per year. Merchant ships may also be a significant source of plastic pellets that have been found in the marine environment. These pellets, used in packaging around larger objects in a ship's hold or to reduce friction on deck during cargo transport, may escape during transit or unloading at port.

Other sources of plastic debris include U.S. Naval and research vessels, passenger vessels and, most importantly, privately owned recreational vessels. In 1984, 9.4 million recreational vessels were registered in the United States with the highest concentrations of these vessels in southern New England, the middle Atlantic, Chesapeake Bay, and the Great Lakes.

Although the disposal of wastes from oil rigs and drilling platforms is strictly regulated, these structures are reportedly a major source of plastic debris. The heaviest concentration of these structures is off the coasts of Louisiana and Texas. In addition to the plastic debris generated by crew members on offshore structures in the Gulf, there are more than 1,000 vessels associated with exploration, development, servicing, production, and product transmission. All of these activities result in the generation of floating or semibuoyant trash and debris.

Land-based sources of plastic debris of particular concern include industries that synthesize plastic and manufacture plastic articles. Sediment samples from rivers, taken below outlet pipes of plastic factories, contain concentrations of plastic pellets in the order of approximately 2,000 pellets per cubic centimeter, suggesting that plastic pellets are directly discharged into the river system by these industries.

In metropolitan areas, primarily along the North Atlantic coast, sewer systems that are combined with storm runoff systems generate large amounts of plastic debris via outfalls in marine areas during times of excess rainfall. Municipal wastewater treatment plants may directly discharge plastic debris from both primary and secondary sewage treatment plants. In the spring of 1976, an estimated 2,200 to 13,000 cubic feet per day of buoyant materials was dumped into the New York Bight area from raw discharges. Sewage sludge dumping in the ocean is also a source of plastic debris. Although buoyant plastic in municipal sewage plants is routinely skimmed during treatment processes, approximately five percent escapes screening and is dumped by barge along with treated sewage sludge. In the late 1970s an estimated 1,000 plastic tampon applicators were dumped with sewage sludge in the New York Bight every day.

Other land-based plastic debris has been attributed to municipal solid waste disposal practices, docks and marinas, and littering by the public.

PRELIMINARY CONCLUSIONS

Evidence is emerging that the disposal of plastic debris in the marine environment is a serious problem for a number of species and for communities and user groups that depend on the marine environment. Even when the information is anecdotal, as it is in many cases, the quantity of such anecdotal reports suggests that the biological and economic impacts may be significant.

Two pieces of legislation were passed in 1987: ratification of Annex V of the MARPOL Treaty, and the Marine Plastic Pollution Research and Control Act of 1987. The U.S. ratified Annex V to the International Convention for the Prevention of Pollution from Ships (MARPOL). The signatory nations agreed that by the beginning of 1989, their ships (including pleasure vessels) will not dump plastic garbage anywhere at sea, nor may vessels of other nations dump plastic garbage in the waters of signatory countries. The Marine Plastic Pollution Research and Control Act enables the U.S. government to enforce Annex V.

Management agencies, at the federal, state, and local levels, are just beginning to become aware of the magnitude of this issue, and have started to direct their efforts toward investigating the biological and economic impacts associated with marine plastic debris in a systematic manner.

Marine Sanctuaries

✝✝✝✝✝✝

Marine sanctuaries are to this nation's ocean resources what the national parks are to our terrestrial landscape. Yellowstone Park, our first national park, was designated in 1872. The U.S.S. Monitor Marine Sanctuary, designated in 1975 to protect the wreck of the Civil War Ironclad *USS Monitor,* was the first designated U.S. marine sanctuary. And since 1975, seven additional marine sanctuaries have been designated protecting other outstanding marine areas. American boaters can regularly enjoy the many moods of our nation's waters. Even so, many boaters are unaware of the rich, living seascape beneath them.

The United States is blessed with more than 2.2 million square miles of ocean under its jurisdiction with an unrivaled diversity of marine habitats and resources. From the oasislike boulder patches of Alaska's Beaufort Sea to the colorful coral reefs of the Florida Keys, the United States possesses an underwater legacy equal to its most spectacular mountain ranges and deserts on land. However, human activity within this vast area is accelerating, particularly in near-shore waters, and some areas are already being damaged.

The primary purpose of the national marine sanctuary program is to conserve nationally significant marine areas through management, research and education. Rather than focusing upon one particular

National Marine Sanctuary Program

North Puget Sound

Western Washington Outer Coast

Cordell Bank

Gulf of the Farallones

Monterey Bay

Channel Islands

Santa Monica Bay

Fagatele Bay

Stellwagen Bank

Norfolk Canyon

U.S.S. Monitor

Gray's Reef

Flower Garden Banks

Key Largo

Alligator Reef

Looe Key

Sombrero Reef

American Shoal

△ Proposed
Ⓢ Congressionally Mandated
● Designated

resource or activity, a marine sanctuary seeks to elevate the conservation of all resources in an area through the coordination that is sometimes lacking among the diverse marine and coastal programs of state and federal agencies.

Before declaring an area a marine sanctuary, the federal government must consult with Congress, state agencies, citizens' groups, and the general public and must determine that—

- the area is of special national significance because of its resources or human-use value;
- existing state and federal authorities are inadequate for comprehensive conservation and management of the area, including resource protection, scientific research, and public education;
- designation of the area as a national marine sanctuary will facilitate such coordinated and comprehensive conservation land management; and
- the area is of a size and nature that will permit this kind of management.

Implementation of the national marine sanctuary program has been fitful. With little fanfare, the program designated two sites in 1975 after which the program languished without an office or funds.

In 1977, President Carter called for accelerated implementation of the program even as his administration pursued accelerated oil and gas development on the outer continental shelf. The program was soon caught up in battles over allowing or prohibiting oil and gas drilling in sensitive marine areas. The oil and gas industry targeted the sanctuary program for elimination.

In a flurry of activity at the end of the Carter administration, four sanctuaries were designated, two of them with oil and gas prohibitions. The incoming Reagan administration froze the oil and gas prohibitions but reinstated them after reluctantly determining that the benefits outweighed the costs of the prohibitions.

Congress reviewed the national marine sanctuary program in 1987 and renewed its commitment to protecting outstanding marine resources. Four new sites have been placed on the active candidate list.

Stellwagen Bank is located between Cape Cod and Cape Ann, Massachusetts. It consists of 605 nautical miles of physical and oceanographic features resulting in unusually high biological productivity and supports large populations of fish and marine mammals. Three species of endangered large whales, the humpback, the fin, and the right whale are found at Stellwagen. In addition, the plentiful food supply at Stellwagen attracts a diverse group of pelagic and coastal birds.

Flower Garden Banks is located 115 miles south of Galveston, Texas, and supports the northernmost shallow-water tropical coral reef in the Gulf of Mexico.

Monterey Bay is located off the central California coast. Monterey Bay has a great diversity of habitats, such as kelp beds, sandy beaches, and several submarine canyons. The Monterey Canyon, which begins less than one mile from shore, is the largest submarine canyon on the North American continental shelf and is deeper than the Grand Canyon of the Colorado River.

Outer Coast in Washington is a near-shore area adjacent to Olympic National Park, which borders one of the least developed shores in North America. The recognition of Olympic National Park as an international biosphere reserve and world heritage site attests to the uniqueness of the area. Offshore rocks provide haulout areas for seals and sea lions and breeding areas for 50 percent of the state's marine birds.

Other sites to be reviewed by the federal government include:

- **North Atlantic:** Mid-Coastal Maine; Nantucket Sound/Shoals and Oceanographer Canyon; Assateague Island, Virginia.
- **South Atlantic:** Ten Fathom Ledge/Big Rock; Port Royal Sound; Florida Coral Grounds.
- **Caribbean:** Cordillera Reefs, Puerto Rico; Southeast St. Thomas, U.S. Virgin Islands; East End, St. Croix, U.S. Virgin Islands.
- **Gulf of Mexico:** Big Bend Seagrass Beds, Florida; Shoalwater Bay/Chandaleur Sound; Baffin Bay, Texas.
- **Eastern Pacific:** Heceta-Stonewall Banks, Oregon; Morro Bay, California; Tanner-Cortes Banks, California.
- **Western Pacific:** Northern Mariana Islands; Southern Mariana Islands; Cocos Lagoon, Guam; Facpi Point to Fort Santo Angel, Guam; Papalola Point, Ofu Island, American Samoa.
- **Great Lakes:** Cape Vincent, Lake Ontario; Western Lake Erie Islands including Sandusky Bay; Thunder Bay, Lake Huron; Green Bay; Apostle Islands/ Isle Royale, Lake Superior.

Only relatively recently have we as a people accorded our marine heritage the level of care and protection that we have given our national parks and wildlife refuges. Hopefully, many of these candidate sites will join the ranks of protected marine sanctuaries and thereby enlarge our legacy of ocean resources for future generations.

Return of the
Prehistoric Creatures

⸙ ⸙ ⸙ ⸙ ⸙ ⸙

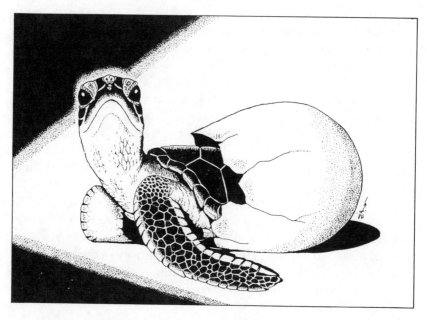

Have you ever wanted to see a prehistoric creature up close? Do you regret being born millions of years too late? Well, take heart. Survivors of the Age of the Dinosaurs are alive and reproducing among us.

Imagine, if you will, an anchorage by a dark and quiet beach. Stars fill the night sky. Palm fronds rustle in the breeze. Waves crash on the shore. A village dog barks in the distance. You have beached the dinghy and have been sitting quietly for over two hours waiting for them to come. There are tracks in the sand, indisputable evidence that some were here last night and the night before that. Your hands and legs are covered with fine black sand, and the ubiquitous sand fleas are beginning to bite. You stare at the place where the waves come in and recede. There is nothing. You wonder if you're ever going to see one. And then . . . it happens.

As the last wave washes in and goes out again there is a creature bigger than the wave ever was but you didn't see her until the wave was gone. She must have made one enormous lunge from the sea. She pauses for a very long moment. Slowly, she begins to drag herself up the beach. You hold very still. You pray that she won't notice you. That she'll just follow her instincts and do what she came ashore to do, just as two million generations before her have done. She doesn't know it, but she's one of the lucky ones. This female has come ashore on a safe beach; she will survive the night.

Each year this scene is repeated thousands of times on tropical beaches the world over as sea turtles come ashore to nest. These ancient reptiles have survived for over 65 million years, but today their very existence is threatened by man. Man has hunted turtles for their meat and skin and oil and shells. He has stolen their eggs. He has polluted the ocean and altered their nesting beaches and foraging areas. Now seven of the world's eight species of sea turtles are considered to be in danger of extinction.

To watch a primitive and vulnerable turtle weighing hundreds of pounds drag herself up the beach to lay her eggs is an unforgettable experience. By observing just a few "rules," you will ensure that the turtle is not disturbed and you and future observers will fully enjoy this wonder of nature.

Sea turtles are fascinating creatures, in large part because we know so little about them. The mystery begins when a hatchling turtle emerges from its nest and disappears into the sea. After (probably) spending its first year in the sargassum weed, the young turtle may move to a coastal area for foraging. The juveniles of some species, such as the leatherback and the olive ridley, are rarely seen. On reaching reproductive age (estimates vary from 15 to 50 years), turtles will return to nest on the beach where they hatched. The ability to find this beach which may be hundreds or thousands of miles away is a mystery. Like other long-distance migrants, sea turtles probably depend on a combination of abilities. Whatever factors are involved, sea turtles are among the earth's greatest ocean navigators.

The beaches of the southeast United States from South Carolina to Florida are prime nesting habitat for the loggerhead sea turtle and, to a lesser extent, green and leatherback turtles. Most female sea turtles breed every second or third year but during a season a female may lay several clutches of eggs at about two week intervals. From May through August it is possible to watch sea turtles nest. In July, about eight weeks after the first nests are laid, the tiny hatchlings begin to emerge. Hatching continues through the end of October. Should you be lucky enough to actually observe an emergence from the ocean, I guarantee that you will be impressed. Watching a loggerhead or green turtle weighing several hundred pounds come from the surf is tantamount to seeing the arrival of the creature from the deep. Even more impressive is the 800- to 1200-pound leatherback, which is likened to a Volkswagen Beetle coming from the sea.

Please remember that sea turtles are protected by the U.S. Endangered Species Act and it is a violation to "take, harass, harm, pursue, hunt" marine turtles, their nests, and/or eggs. The penalty can range up to a $50,000 fine and one year of imprisonment.

Sea turtle nesting takes place in several stages: emergence, excavation of the body pit, excavation of the egg chamber, egg laying, covering of the nest, and return to the sea.

Exceedingly vulnerable on land, sea turtles are quite skittish when they emerge from the ocean to nest. To avoid frightening away a potential nester, it is advisable not to be too close to the shoreline. Remain still and at a distance as the female emerges and chooses her nesting spot. Nesting takes place in several stages over an hour or two. First the female will excavate a body pit—beware of flying sand. Some species, such as the green turtle, dig a pit up to two feet deep. The next stage is the preparation of a flask-shaped egg chamber. To accomplish this, the female digs with her hind flippers, alternating one and then the other flipper until they can reach no more. You can approach quietly from behind as she digs the egg chamber. After the chamber is complete, the eggs are released in small clusters of two or three at a time from the females's cloaca.

Approximately the size of ping-pong balls, the egg shells are white and look like leather. The average clutch size is 120 eggs but that number can vary considerably. It is recommended that you leave your flashlight off at all times. If you do want to see the eggs more clearly, briefly turn your light on and off again. Your eyes will adjust rapidly to the dark. Remember not to touch the turtle or her eggs. Beware again of flying sand as the turtle covers the eggs and returns to the sea. With luck, the eggs will incubate for 50 to 60 days. Turtle nests are vulnerable to a number of predators, such as raccoons and ghost crabs and, in many areas of the world, to humans. Predation is generally highest in the first few days after the nest is laid and right before the hatchlings emerge. The little turtles hatch several days before they emerge from their nest. Activity within the nest causes the sand over-head to fall, slowly raising the level of the nest. When the sand temperatures are cool, the hatchlings break out. They find the sea by heading in the direction of the brightest light, which on a naturally dark beach is the light reflected from the water. Once again the cycle begins as the hatchlings swim away. Some will return one day to nest. If you should see hatchlings struggling on a beach, please remember that it is illegal to touch them and that hatchlings have managed on their own for millions of years. Probably only one in 1,000 will survive to reproduce, but they have been doing that successfully for countless generations. If we leave them alone and stop befouling their habitat, they will continue to survive.

I like to think that with good will and good science, sea turtles and people can use and enjoy the beaches together.

Index

✝ ✝ ✝ ✝ ✝ ✝